I'M PROBABLY GOING TO HELL FOR THIS!

I'm Probably Going to Hell for This!

SCOTT MOSS

swm publishing

CONTENTS

~ 1 ~

I'm pretty sure I'm going to hell for this!
By Scott Moss
Introduction
What is it we all seek? Some sort of reassurance that there is an afterlife. What is it we rely on for that guidance to get us there? Religion. I realize I'm probably going to piss a few people off with this book, but what the hell, if there is a purgatory, I'm sure I'll pay for it there. You see this book came about because of unanswered questions. Questions I've pondered for my 62 years on this earth (minus my time in diapers where thinking was completely optional). Religion in many ways is a guide to obtain answers, but it was never enough for me.

I was raised Catholic. You can all bless me now. Surviving a Catholic upbringing is a lot like surviving a repetitive hurricane. Just when you think you've got enough protection from the danger someone (Usually my Mother) throws a curve ball of Catholic guilt at you and you're stuck trying to remember if it is a sin or not, whether it requires a confession, and the amount of shame you should feel. It's like dodging the hurricane all over again.

Depression runs rough shot in the Catholic religion and trust me, I know why. Happiness is frowned upon. I have a hard time thinking that God thinks that's the way it should be.

Although I am by no means an expert on religion. I find it to be a hindrance in my life. I do know that a lot of people get a lot out of the visit to the church on Sunday and I think that's great. By no means do I think that everyone should follow my lead, I just want people to know that being a religious truant is not the end of the world. I have always felt that God watches over us. I also think that he (or She, oh that's going to piss off some people) wants us to be happy. I can't see a God that punishes people for eating a beef jerky on a Friday during lent and yet forgiving a murderer because he confesses his sin on his deathbed. Sorry, it just doesn't work for me.

So as you go through this book realize that I have a sense of humor and I will let it loose here. I believe God has one too. It's easy to see in some circumstances. If you are a balding man and are now growing more hair on your back then on your head, that may be God playing a little joke on you or at least getting you back for all the time you spent in front of the mirror making sure your full head of hair was perfect. He's funny that way. I was thin and in good physical shape when I was in my early 20's. Girls actually looked at me occasionally. I got married at 22 and my wife refused to gain any weight during the 4 pregnancies we had, so I was forced (maybe by God) to do it for her. Now the only reason a women looks at me is to wonder what big and tall shop makes jeans that large.

Now let's get this started.

Chapter One

In the Beginning

The first thing I want to say is that the Big Bang Theory is not only a fantastic TV show it's also the common belief in how the universe was formed. Now here's where things get tricky. Did God light the fuse? Did he just lay back and watch things develop for a few billion years and then get to work? Maybe he has a vacation home in heaven that he spent some time at to gather his thoughts on how this whole thing should go. He let the universe spread out and cool down and then looked around for the perfect setting to drop us in. Earth seemed like a good place for us. It had potential after the dinosaurs kicked off. Water, food, caves, instant fire from a lightning strike. Let's face it, it had it all. He saw the beaches and said, "What a great place for overpriced condos" and looked down at the Midwest and said "who forgot to put the majestic mountains I ordered down there? Looks like will just have to grow corn and soybeans."

I know some of you out there are angry that I left out the possibility that God created the heaven and Earth in six days and rested on the seventh. The reason I find this hard to believe is, if God can do anything he wants then why rush the process? Why not take your time and make things like Hawaii and the French Alps look as good as they do. Six days just doesn't cut it. I can't get a pothole in my town patched in six days. Why would God rush things? Take your time, isn't that what all the good teachers say? And if he did create the universe in six days it's obvious, he wasn't in a union. No scheduled breaks and no mention of overtime on Saturday. Maybe God needed a good union representative, and no one was available. Sometimes it's rough being number 1. No help from anyone. You're on your own no matter what.

What kind of rest did God take on the seventh day? Did he sleep in till 11:00? Maybe watch some football? Order a pizza from the future? Hit the sack early? It's a visual you have to really think about. I'm also thinking God has the biggest flat screen TV ever made. If you're going to rest, go big. What did he do on Monday? Right back to work? Maybe designed a few new trees and slipped in a couple of new species? Did he need extra coffee to get going that morning due to all the major stuff he did the week before? And I have another question. Does God have a desk? I'd imagine it would be a real nice one. A nice flip calendar that starts with the date "day 1" on it and as time goes by, he tears off the dates and tosses them in the gold garbage can. I guess we won't know until we get there.

The hard thing to contemplate is the same question that is asked over and over again. Does God have any construction skills? I don't know about you, but I have a hard time nailing two 2x4's together. Building a universe would require quite a bit of architectural skill, how planets orbit, and of course how to turn a tree into a 2x4. The earth required quite a large amount of geometry too. I had some serious issues with geometry. God obviously did not. He has great knowledge that's pretty obvious. But you can only know so much about everything. I think that may explain some of the things that happened in the early beginnings of our earth. We started off really hot. Earth was covered with lava. God came down and tried to plant some trees and realized he needed to make some changes. He started throwing comets filled with ice at the planet to cool it off. But that didn't happen overnight. I can imaging God zooming through the universe redirecting all the comets toward earth in hopes of cooling it off. He probably invented baseball that way. Just up there whipping comets at the earth like it was a catcher's mitt. Before you know it, we've got trees and God is happy. But then something happened. God must have bumped the thermostat and we plunged into an age where the entire earth was covered with ice.

Now God being the go-getter he is, he had to figure out a way to warm things up again. It took millions of years, but before you knew it...trees again! By the way, I'm making this stuff up based on the shows I've watched on the Discovery Channel and it's pretty obvious I haven't watched them in any sort of order. Don't quote me on these historic times in earth's evolution because you'll just piss off the geologists, paleontologists, and physicists. I guess I could go look it up, but it requires me to search the internet and even God doesn't have time for that. I'll end up at some site that God would not approve of...like www.ilovesandrabullock.com. By the way a side note. God was playing his "A" game when he made her. Sorry, off on a tangent.

So, God gets things pretty much the way he wants them but makes a little mistake that will hinder man's development on earth. Dinosaurs. Angry beasts that would snack on us like I do on Twinkie's. So, after at least a couple of million years of putting up with that, he had had enough. He sent a comet or asteroid or a big meteorite or for all we know a very large baseball down to the earth causing a massive explosion and lots of dust to block out the sun. That was all for the dinosaurs. Soon things cleared up and God was sure that it was almost time to put us on earth and get things rolling.

Even though evolution is frowned upon in the religious community we do have some evidence that it occurred. They call them "Fossils" and I've seen a few so I know they're real. Gods sending of man down to earth started of like Microsoft version of Windows. The first draft was rough around the edges and crashed a lot, but as time went on the user interface became quite complex. Man 3.1 looked about two steps away from Gorilla 10.0. God liked gorillas but it wasn't what he had in mind for us. He kept upgrading. Man 3.1, 3.2, and so on. He reached Windows Vista with Neanderthal man. If you had Windows Vista, you knew it worked but at any moment things could get ugly. Finally, he caught up to Microsoft and developed Human 9.0 and God was pleased.

Now we've looked all over the world to find the oldest human remains. Turns out, God liked Africa better than all the other continents. Now from a biblical sense, this changes things quite dramatically. If there was a Garden of Eden and an Adam and Eve, the garden was in Africa, and Adam and Eve were probably black. Oh, great now I pissed off the KKK. And I have a phobia of white sheets. Not to mention all the Renaissance painters. But why couldn't Adam and Eve be black? We'll all know someday, and I can't wait to see the look on all the prejudice people in the world faces. Priceless.

I think God put a form of man on earth and let us evolve on our own. Some of us made it, some not. I would not have. I'm way too fat to outrun a saber tooth tiger. And finding an animal skin to fit me would be tough too. No big and tall shops back then. So God let man evolve into the species we are today. And I think he's still letting us evolve. Some faster than others. Congress would be a good example of the ones evolving slowly; caring, loving mothers are evolving faster. It's really a crap shoot. Come on 7!

For argument's sake, let's say after all those years of evolution God picked two people to assume the role of Adam and Eve. He made them a nice garden with an "all-you-can-eat buffet" and plenty of things to do. I know this story is deeper than that with people like Lilith and her banishment from the garden for not being submissive to Adam which of course was the beginning of the oppression of women. Who knows, maybe Lilith was a nice girl who just wanted a little freedom to start her own business or make some decisions about decorating the garden. This didn't sit well with God or Adam who obviously teamed up against her. She was kicked out of the garden with a significant punishment involving dead babies. 100 at a time, every day. I don't know who the obstetrician was back then, but I'm sure they didn't get much sleep. I find the story of Lilith to be one of mystery and downright discrimination. Let's hope God and Adam have apologized to her and she is happy now in heaven.

Let's talk a little about Eve. Made from the rib of Adam. Here in Chicago, there is a restaurant called "Adam's Ribs". Every time you order the ribs you get a free wife and complimentary coleslaw. I'm not too sure about this, I haven't been there. But back to the question at hand. Did God come down and do a quick ribectomy on Adam to create Eve? I'm assuming that being God will allow you to practice medicine without a license is not a big deal. (I feel a lightning bolt coming on). This amazing feat was completed while Adam slept in the Garden. Now waking up with a very sore rib cage is a small price to pay to see a beautiful naked woman lying next to you. I'm sure Adam quickly managed to ignore the pain. According to the paintings of the past, Eve was the equivalent of a supermodel. Adam must have had a very special rib.

Now we have Adam and Eve. They could have anything they wanted in the garden except the fruit from this one tree. I'm assuming that the garden had everything. So why did Eve feel the need to tempt Adam with the "Forbidden Fruit"? Although it states in the bible that the Devil had something to do with it, I wonder if Eve wanted a bigger garden with a mansion and several servants and assumed she could do better if they left God's garden. Big Mistake. Things got ugly right after they bit into the forbidden fruit. I won't go into the details but let's say that Eve didn't get what she wanted. Don't get me wrong, I don't think it was just Eve's fault. Adam must have dreamed of a fancy car and a nice speed boat. They got greedy. It is still a fault we all suffer from today.

So, the couple gets evicted from the garden. They wander until they find a nice two-story cave with curtains and an above-ground pool in the back. They decide to start a family and have at least two sons. Cain and Able. I'm not sure if they had daughters but if you believe that they were the start of civilization, some sisters had to be around. This also confuses me. We all know that marrying your sister is a big no-no. It's even worse to have children with her. The kids won't come out the way you want them. That's just basic chromosomal facts. But I guess if God is running the show and has gotten over the whole "Garden of Eden" debacle, he could allow normal children to be born from these unions.

As you know, no family is perfect. There's always one jerk. Sometimes more. In the case of the first family, it was Cain. He obviously had a temper and was not invited to most of the family gatherings. Cain had to sit at the kids table long after Able was allowed to sit at the adult table and a sibling rivalry was born. Cain got his opportunity to exact his revenge and killed Able with a very large rock. As I do recall this didn't work out too well for Cain, and he was never invited back for family get-togethers.

Chapter two

We got people now!

As the population grew and people spread out things started to get worse. There were terrible things going on. Strip clubs, prostitution, worshiping false Gods, and of course, politicians. People had forgotten about God and his rules. Except for one. This man's name was Noah. Noah was minding his own business when he got a call on the hot line from God. God said "Noah! I want you to build an Ark". And in what has to be one of the funniest lines in all of the comedy written by Bill Cosby, Noah said "Right. What's an Ark"? Then God gave Noah the architectural plan for the Arc in a measure of cubits. Noah then asked, "What's a cubit"? And God had to give Noah a quick lesson in measurements, naval building, and I hope, some sort of sanitation system for the arc. Noah spent many years building the arc without one permit from the city. His neighbors complained that it was an eyesore. After completion of the arc, Noah was instructed to find two of every animal on earth (Male and female, very important in the overall scheme of things) and put them in the arc. This is where the story loses its possibilities with me. It takes years to acquire all the animals for a good zoo. And yet they don't have them all. The arc would have to be the size of Connecticut to do all this. And what about the flying animals? Aren't they going to take the first oppor-tunity to fly out a window as soon as Noah opens one to air the place out? The logistics of this undertaking are mind-boggling when you get into it. What about insects? You can't put the lions anywhere near the wildebeests, can you? You have to separate the snakes and the mice. You have to reinforce the area of the arc where the elephants and rhinos are being kept. I'm sorry. I just can't believe that this is more than just a fable to show God's power. Everybody's misbehaving, so let's flood the earth and save only one family and all the animals. I'm sure some of you believe it, but it is one of the stories in the bible that I just don't have much faith in. I think it's a great story to get the point across that God can take everything away in a moment of anger. I just have a hard time with it.

The world slowly repopulates and God is in a much better mood. Things seem to be going well with the world. Abraham came along and God and he talked. He said, "Let's move". I don't like this neighborhood anymore. Abraham moved his people to Florida where they all retired and drove Buicks up on the sidewalk. I don't know what made me say that. I'm sure I'll make time for that statement too. They were instructed to obtain their own land in Canaan. At least that's what I understand. This is the part of the Old Testament that confuses me the most. The war years. When God O.K.'d the savage destruction of several groups of people so the Israelites could have their own land. Doesn't seem like God would just up and O.K. that kind of violence. Maybe it's just me, but unless someone's completely out of control (Like Napoleon, Hitler, or Saddam Husain) God wouldn't approve of any kind of mass murder even if the people didn't believe in his existence. Maybe these were incredibly bad people with poor credit scores and bad attitudes, but still, there are passages in the bible that talk of total destruction of all of the people. Including women and children. I think this was just men who had great ambition and used God as their excuse to wipe out a country so they could obtain its riches and land. So many people died in the name of God. I don't think he would like the association.

Chapter 3

Abraham was probably the most tested of God's prophets. He dreamed of having a son to take over the family business of running God's world for him. But his wife Sarah was barren. So Sarah offered an Egyptian handmaiden, Hagar, for Abram to consort with so that he may have a child by her, as a wife. Now I don't know about you, but I would have a hard time having a baby with a woman named Hagar. I'm sure it's just because of the comic strip, but still, Hagar? Ishmael was born to Abraham and Hagar when Abraham was 86 years old. Way to go Abraham! But it didn't stop there. An angel told Sarah she would have a baby. She was 90 years old, and Abraham was 100. What were they putting in the water back then? Maybe they didn't count years the way we do, but something seems awfully strange in this story. Isaac was born to Abraham and Sarah and he became the next chosen leader of the Israelites. Abraham was given a test when Isaac was a boy when God told him to take Isaac up to the mountain and sacrifice him. The guy waits 100 years for a son and then God wants him back? I understand the testing of one's faith but this is out of the ballpark. So, Isaac goes with Dad probably thinking there's a Chucky Cheese at the top of the mountain. Instead, he gets tied up, and placed on a makeshift altar, and just as Abraham is about to stab him, an angel appears with a nice little lamb to sacrifice instead of Isaac. No, I'm thinking if there were Psychiatrists back then Isaac would be entitled to free sessions for at least 10 years to get over this trauma. Now it even gets more interesting from here. Sarah passed away (can you blame her) and Abraham had six more sons with Hagar. This guys a machine. He finally passed away (I'm sure from pure exhaustion) at the age of 175.

Let's skip ahead a little to Sodom and Gomorra. Now this is an interesting story. God's angry again. Seems like the people of the two towns have been more than a little bit bad. Wild orgies, prostitution running wild, and no respect for God's laws. God scans both towns with his special powers and finds only one family that is good enough to avoid his anger. Lot is our man. He and his family are instructed by the warrior angel to quickly get out of the city and don't look back. So, Lot quickly gets his family to the subway and takes the purple line out of town. No? Alright, he ran out of the city instructed by the angels not to look back at the city while it is being destroyed. Lots wife, obviously not a good listener, glances back at the city and is quickly turned into a pillar of salt. Now I know Lot was a good man who obeyed God. But I think he had to be a little angry with him at that moment. It seems a little harsh to me. Maybe break her leg or give her a nasty case of boils, but a pillar of salt? Now Lot is a widower and has to try to find another wife. The kids are confused and no matter what they say to mommy, she won't answer. Another day in purgatory for me.

By the way, just so you know this is not in any strict order. I'm winging it based on what I remember and how it sometimes makes sense to me and sometimes does not. There may be explanations for things like Sarah having a baby at 90 years old. I don't know. But if God can get that done, I'm sure he can do almost anything. The reason I say almost is he couldn't teach me algebra. In fact, spell check just corrected me on the word algebra, so I think it's fair to say it is one of his few failures.

So, let's move along. Isaac became the next leader but his role in the early beginnings is kind of confusing to me. He is considered to be one of the patriarchs and is a saint, but the information on him is a little shaky. I say that because I am confused by it. That doesn't mean I believe his role was unimportant. And I just read that when Abraham took him up to the mountain to sacrifice him, he was 37 years old. Seems like he could have put up a fight being that would make his father 137. This Abraham guy was amazing! Probably had his black belt. Isaac lived even longer than his father, making it to 180 years old. I wonder if he outlived his pension. I guess it depends on what union he was in. Were the teamsters around back then?

Now Jacob was the son of Isaac. He was taking a walk one day and as night approached, he pulled up a rock, put it under his head (obviously, the pillow had not been invented yet), and fell asleep. He dreamed of a ladder from Earth to the heavens. Angels were going up and down the ladder ascending and descending to and from heaven. Now I think that this was a very special dream showing how God's workers are always coming down to earth to help us. And the ones going back up to heaven must be on break. There is one thing that bothers me. That ladder must have been somewhat unsafe. God knows of future events, so why didn't he put in an escalator? Much more efficient and has less worry of falling. Maybe some nice music pumped into the escalator area. But I guess an escalator would be a little hard for Jacob to understand

and also, there is the issue of renaming the story "Jacobs' Escalator" which just doesn't flow like Jacob's ladder.

Now Jacob must have felt responsible for repopulating the earth. He had so many children it's hard to keep track of them all. He had 12 sons and one daughter. I hope he had more than one bathroom in his house. Before the birth of Benjamin, Jacob is renamed "Israel" by God. God liked to change the names of his people. It's kind of a running theme in the Old Testament. I'm not sure why, maybe he just didn't like the names given by the parents. Maybe God will rename me after this book comes out. I'm not looking forward to what he names me. I guess it all depends on whether or not he has a sense of humor. But if people start calling me Edna or Gertrude, we can pretty much be sure he was mad.

The next big name in the bible is Joseph. Not Joseph the father or stepfather of Jesus. This is another Joseph. Joseph was a man of many talents. His abilities in dealing with the Egyptian Pharaoh were legendary. He came up with the idea of storing grain for the years when Egypt was affected by famine. For his knowledge, Pharaoh made him second in command over all of Egypt. This was in the good old days when you didn't need a master's degree to move up in the business world. All this and at the time only 30 years old. If Joseph had a car at Pharaoh's palace, he'd have his own parking space and a corner office. Joseph had family problems. It appears his stepbrothers were very jealous and wanted him dead. This makes the holidays very tense. Joseph eventually makes amends with his brothers and holidays are fun again. Joseph lived to be 110. For that time, that is relatively young according to the bible. He must have been a smoker.

Let's skip ahead to one of the biggest names in a bunch of religions. Moses. Now here's an all-around guy. Moses was born a Hebrew and during his infancy, an unknown Pharaoh decreed that all male Hebrew children be drowned in the Nile River. I have a feeling this particular pharaoh has a seat in the fire pit next to Hitler. Moses' mother hid him as long as she could but eventually realized she would have to take a chance and send him down the Nile in a basket. Moses must have had some navigation skills at an early age because he ended up at the Pharaoh's palace. Pharaoh's sister noticed the little boat and had the child brought to her. She raised Moses as an Egyptian. He became a great builder. (according to the movie). But on a day when Moses was walking through a building sight, he saw an Egyptian beating a Hebrew worker and Moses lost it. He beat the Egyptian to death and buried his body in the sand. Unfortunately, Moses forgot the cardinal rule for murdering an Egyptian slave master...make sure there are no witnesses. He knew Pharaoh would find out and put him to death. So Moses got the heck out of dodge and made a long trip through the desert and found a nice family with sheep and their very own well. You can only imagine how thirsty Moses must have been. It was in Midian that Moses protected 7 shepherdesses from a gang of angry shepherds. I'm not sure what a gang of angry shepherds looks like, but I can imagine they wore similar colors and had gang signs to identify each other. But Moses took care of them, and the girl's father took him in as his son. He married one of the daughters named Zipporah. They put monogrammed towels in their bathroom and set up shop. Moses lived in Midian for 40 years as a shepherd and used sheep salesmen. (Feeling another lightning bolt coming on).

Moses took a walk one day up a mountain and saw a burning bush that wasn't being consumed by the flames. The burning bush identified itself as God. Moses asked for some I.D. but God had left it in his other pants. Moses took his word for it and God gave him an assignment that would be refused by most people. God told Moses he would give him the powers needed to free his people from the bondage of the Egyptians and lead them to the Promised Land. Moses asked what the job paid, and God gave him a dirty look. Moses got the hint and went down the mountain with a new assignment. Before long, Moses was back in Egypt making trouble for Pharaoh. He demanded that Pharaoh let his people go. Pharaoh, being the jerk that he was said no. Moses decided to flex a little God muscle and started dropping some plagues on Egypt. He turns the Nile into a river of blood. Drops Frogs, lice and flies on them, kills the cattle, and gives people boils, (and I must remind you, they didn't have Clearasil back then). The last one was the worst. Moses said that the last plague would be from Pharaoh's mouth. Pharaoh told his soldiers to kill all the firstborn children of Israel. Moses reworded the order and substituted Israel with Egyptian, and things got pretty nasty after that. Pharaoh lost his first born and it made him so mad he told Moses to take his people and leave Egypt. So, the Israelites packed up and left Egypt.

Now I have a question before we go on any further. When Moses went to Egypt did he tell his wife he was going on a business trip and was it tax deductible? The women of biblical times were much more understanding of their husbands when they decided to take off for a little adventure across the desert. They left for war and sometimes came back 20 years later. Now I know my wife loves me, but if I left for 20 years, she'd have a line of men waiting for her to give up on me. Not to mention that after 20 years, my looks will surely have faded, and I would no longer be the Hollywood leading man I am now. Stop laughing. I can hear you all the way to my house.

So back to Moses. Moses is leading his people back to the promised land when Pharaoh has a change of heart and decides to kill all the Israelites but to bring Moses back to him so he can kill him. Moses doesn't have a compass and unfortunately finds himself backed up against the sea. God, who isn't happy at all about this turn of events puts up a wall of fire to stop the Egyptians from getting to the Israelites and Moses knows something drastic has to be done. There are no boats available for a leisurely trip across the sea to escape. (It was yacht season) so Moses slams his staff into the water of the red sea, and it opens up leaving a convenient road with several places to get fresh fish and a nice lunch on the way. There is a Target and a Lowe's to help replenish the supplies needed to keep the wagons going and Moses puts it all on Gods credit card. This angers God because the interest rate is astronomical. Moses apologizes and says he'll cover the interest. They barely make it out of the sea because some of the women were lingering in the swimsuit section of Target and Moses had to shoe them out of there.

God's wall of flames was starting to die down and the chariots started to enter the parted sea and try to catch up with the Israelites. They were exceeding the speed limit and were stopped by several of God's angels who wrote them very expensive tickets. Yet this didn't slow them down. They had almost reached the Israelites, and Moses was getting a little aggravated that it was taking them so long to get out of the sea. Just as the last one hit the shore the sea crashed in on Pharaoh's army killing all of them and destroying the Target and Lowes.

Moses heads towards the Mount Sinai area where he had heard they were building nice condo villages with pools and a great mountain view. Turns out condos hadn't been invented yet and there was little water in the desert for a multitude of swimming pools. Moses was called by God to ascend Mount Sinai because God wanted to have a talk with him. Moses was worried because he thought God was mad at him for something he had done in the third grade involving putting tacks on the teacher's chair. Turns out God had forgiven him for that many years ago and was just interested in giving him his new and shiny laws to help govern the people of Israel.

The Ten Commandments are pretty straight forward, and God invented the first laser to burn them into two tablets so Moses could bring them down from the mountain and give them to his people so they could live in harmony and avoid long legal trials. Moses was gone for 40 days and 40 nights. That only makes sense. If you're going to be gone that long you might as well get the hotel points and stay the extra night. But there were problems going on down in the camp. It would appear that everyone got tired of waiting for Moses thinking maybe he had bought one of those previous condos I mentioned and was sitting poolside working on his tan. They made a golden calf and started worshiping it as their new God. Now being that the first commandment says "I am the Lord thy God. You shall have no other Gods before me". Whoops on the golden calf thing. As Moses got to his people after descending the mountain they were dancing around the calf and sinning big time. Moses who was known for his short fuse threw the commandments down to the groundbreaking them into lots of pieces. Then he had a good talking to his people. They repented, and because Crazy Glue had not been invented yet to put the tablets back together, Moses was forced to go back up the mountain and get another set from God. God wasn't happy thinking Moses should have been more careful, but he of course remembered the commandments and whipped up another set for Moses. Then he stored them on his computer just in case Moses lost his temper again. Moses took the copies down to his people and this time they welcomed him with open arms and agreed to follow the commandments. But God was still a little angry. So, he made the Israelites wander in the desert for 40 years until all of the previous sinners were dead and gone. Moses got a reprieve because he wasn't at the party. So did his brother Aaron. After 40 years they were finally brought to the Promised Land but Moses was not allowed to go there because he was told to hit a rock once with his staff so it would produce water for his thirsty people. Like most humans, when hitting the rock didn't work immediately, Moses hit it again. This made God mad and he punished Moses by not letting him enter the Promised Land. Seems a little harsh to me. Moses wandered the desert for 40 years and just because he hit a rock twice instead of once he can't enter the Promised Land? God must have been having a bad day that day.

Moses reached the river Jordan but had to stay on the eastern side of it because God was still angry about the rock thing. They sang him a song or two, Moses prayed for his people and then wandered up Mount Nebo and died. He was 120 years old. God is said to have buried him. This part is interesting to me. God wouldn't let him into the promised land but was willing to do the back-breaking work of digging his grave and putting him into it. I'm sure God has angels who could do that for him. Maybe God felt bad about the rock thing and decided this would be a good way to honor Moses' achievements. I'm sure I'll find out someday. Or if God reads this book, maybe not.

Now this is where Joshua takes over. He was Moses' assistant (You think they would have at least given him the title of Vice President). He led the Israelite tribes in the conquest of Canaan. Now here's another blood bath I don't understand. If you're going to let your people wander for 40 years, would you send them in a direction so they would find some fertile ground that wasn't occupied by a group of people? Sometimes this war thing is very hard for me to understand. But anyway, Joshua quickly dispensed of the Canaanites and the Israelites moved in. According to biblical chronology Joshua lived between 1355-1245 BCE or sometime in the late Bronze Age.

The Battle of Jericho is a battle in the biblical Book of Joshua, (Joshua 6:1-27) the first battle of the Israelites during their conquest of Canaan. According to the narrative, the walls of Jericho fell after Joshua's Israelite army marched around the city blowing their trumpets. Now I'm not an expert on trumpets but being able to knock down a wall with a bunch of them is pretty impressive. These guys must have played as well as Dizzy Gillespie. Alright, I'm sure God had a hand in it too. Joshua took the city, and it became home. Joshua lived to be about 110 and I'm not sure about what they ate in biblical times, but everyone lived long lives. Joshua was believed to be a profit.

Now let's talk a little about Samson. When I was a kid, this was one of my favorite stories. Samson was born to a woman named Manoah who thought she was barren. She is told by angels never to cut his hair because his strength is derived from it. I'm sure the other kids made fun of him but being that they lived very far from a "Supercuts", Samson's mother did what she was told and Samson's hair grew long and his strength grew greater. He was drafted by the Bears in the first round and played 10 seasons for them until in a freak ceiling fan incident, Samson lost his hair and his starting spot on the Bears front line.

Samson was more than strong. He was a great warrior. Killing thousands of Philistines using unconventional weapons such as the jawbone of an ass. This had to be very embarrassing for the Philistines, and I'm sure several generals were demoted. But Samson isn't all together when it comes to women. He has bad luck picking them and his first wife is Philistine. This angers the Philistine establishment, and they burn her and her father to death. As you can imagine this angers Samson greatly and he kills more Philistines. After that he retreats to a cave where the Israelites find him and tell him "Hey, quit killing Philistines or they will kill all of us. Come with us and turn yourself in". Samson agrees and they tie him up. He breaks free and grabs the jawbone of an ass (something that must have been just laying around in the street) and kills a thousand Philistines.

Later, Samson falls in love with a bad girl named Delilah. She seduces him and Sampson, being like most of us men, falls for it. She eventually gets him to talk about his strength and Sampson mistakenly makes it known to her that it is given to him by his long hair. While Samson sleeps Delilah cuts his hair (She wasn't a licensed beautician, so the haircut wasn't very good). When Samson awakes, he has no strength. He's angry with Delilah and tells her he will no longer take her to her favorite restaurant for steak. Just then a Philistine leader enters the room and gives Delilah 1100 pieces of silver. She, like many New York housewives takes the money and runs. Samson has his eyes poked out and is forced to do manual labor.

The Philistines decide to sacrifice Samson to one of their Gods and strap him to the pillars in their temple. The temple is packed because it's bingo night and everyone is staying to play after the sacrifice. Samson sees (Poor choice of words). Samson asks God for the strength to destroy the temple and everyone in it including himself.

Samson knocks down the pillars that support the building causing it to crumble and kill all the bingo enthusiasts. They don't know if Delilah was in the building but being that she had 1100 pieces of silver to play with, a lot of people think she was killed too. Samson, I'd like to party with this guy.

Next on my incomplete list is Samuel. Also, a prophet and a all-around good guy except for the time he executed the king of the Amalekites. Sometimes even a prophet can get a little angry and lose it. Samuel is known mainly for anointing King Saul and King David. Before David was king he killed Goliath while in Saul's army. We'll get into that later. Saul was a good king for the first part of his reign but then got greedy and ended up out of favor with God. Samuel was instructed to anoint David as future king and Saul wasn't too happy about it. He became paranoid of David believing that all David wanted was his crown. David was loyal to Saul and didn't take over till after Saul's death on the battlefield.

David and Goliath is one of the stories of the bible that just about everyone knows. David was a used car salesman and Goliath was looking for a nice Cadillac because of his size (6'9" according to most biblical accounts). David tried to sell him a Honda Civic because it had been on the lot for a long time. Goliath got mad and David and he went at it. Another day in purgatory for that one. Goliath was a Philistine who challenged Saul and the Israelites every day for 40 days (Why is 40 days so prominent in the bible)? He wanted Saul to send out his best warrior to fight him and the battle would be decided by the outcome. David was just a boy who was like John Wayne with a sling. David asked Saul if he could fight him, and Saul thought he was dipping into the sacred wine a little too much. Saul finally relented and offered David his armor but David refused. He takes only his sling and 5 stones from a nearby river. Goliath seeing David approach starts to say nasty things about his mother and tells him to go back to pre-school. David starts whipping his sling around and sends a stone right into Goliath's forehead knocking him out. David rushes up to him and cuts his head off with Goliath's own sword. The Philistines run for cover and David is given great favor in Saul's army from that day forward. Goliath retires after the battle being that he didn't have a head. Saul made David a commander over his armies and offered him his daughter Michal in marriage for bringing 100 fore-skins of the Philistines but David brought back 200, saying "God was with me." Now I'm assuming that there was a reason for picking foreskins over something easier to cut off such as a hand or a foot. I don't know what that reason is, but you have to feel sorry for the army when they were given this assignment. I'm sure there was some trouble in the ranks, and David was forced to lay down the law to get them to do what they were told. But I'm curious why David felt the need to be an overachiever and bring back two hundred. Wasn't one hundred enough? It would have impressed the hell out of me. And who's responsible for counting the said foreskins? Another job that was prob-ably given to a lowly private. O.K. that's enough foreskin talk. David was successful in many battles, and his popu-larity awakened Saul's fears.

Eventually, David becomes a great King and wins many battles except one. We'll get into that a little later. He brings a time of great prosperity to the people of Israel and wins many battles. David is thought to be responsible for many of the psalms that are written in the bible. He was also a great musician playing electric guitar with Jimi Hendrix's ancestors. David brought the Ark of the Covenant to Jerusalem, intending to build a temple.

There was this hot babe on the roof of her house taking a bath. Her name was Bathsheba. (Hence the bath part). She is the wife of one of King David's most loyal soldiers Uriah. Uriah is away in a holy war and men fighting a holy war are not allowed to have sex. David seduces her even though she says she's loyal to her husband. (An on-going theme through history). Bathsheba becomes pregnant with David's child. David calls for Uriah to meet with him and offer him a night at home with his lovely wife Bathsheba to cover up the baby's true father, David. Uriah, being the God-fearing man he was, doesn't sleep with Bathsheba because of the holy war he's involved in. King David gets angry and sends him to the front where he is quickly killed. The baby is born but David is punished for his indiscretions and the baby dies. God does grant him more children with his eight wives (imagine the fighting going on in that house) and the one who inherits his kingdom is Solomon. David becomes bedridden and dies. He is buried at Mount Zion.

The whole time all of this is going on there are holy wars being fought everywhere. A little factoid here. Did you know more people have been killed over the years due to religious battles than all other wars combined? Seems like a lot of killing to get your religion to the top of the heap. As you can tell I'm not a big believer in religion in general. But if you get something out of it, then I think it's a good thing. Just my opinion, that's what happens when you write a book.

Solomon was next in line. Now out of all the prophets I researched King Solomon is by far the most confusing. The first thing you should know is that he reined from 970-931 B.C. according to some accounts. So very little archeological evidence can be found. But more importantly, and by far the most amazing thing I found in the stories of Solomon, is the fact that he had 700 wives and 300 concubines. Now I have had only one wife in the last 30 years and sometimes (Forgive me honey) things can get a little rocky. Now multiply that by 700. And add the 300 concubines to the picture and you've got a big mess on your hands. Now let's look at the numbers. If he truly was "involved" with all these women, the math is astonishing. If Solomon had "relations" with all these women, let's say to the tune of 3 a day, that means that the concubines would get to have sex with Solomon only once a year and the wives only a little over twice a year. Now I know the sex drive of men is higher than women's, but I have a feeling some of his wives and concubines had other men on the side. You just can't keep all those women happy and try to run a kingdom at the same time. Although my hat is off to Solomon, he had it going on. Women were one of his weaknesses, but if you're going to have a weakness, that's not a bad one to have. I've asked my wife about the wives and concubines, and she said I would have to limit them to 70 and 30. A much more manageable amount. There's a good chance I would know most of their names and I would have to somehow clone myself, which is greatly frowned upon in most religions. And I'm definitely going to have to get a better job. But that will leave little time for my harem. Maybe they should support me as they did Solomon. They brought gold and other riches from their kingdoms so I guess I could live off of that. It's all so simple...NOT!

Solomon is also famous for a story that intrigues me. Two women approached him to settle an argument about a baby. They both said the baby was theirs and were fighting for possession like two basketball players fighting for the ball. Solomon, having great wisdom but a lousy sense of anatomy and the workings of the human body, offered to divide the child in half and give each woman one half. The first woman said that would be just fine (also showing her lack of the body's natural need for all the organs to function properly) if Solomon divided the child down the middle. The second woman said she would rather give up the child than see it killed by said division. Solomon knew that her compassion for the child meant she was the true mother and gave her the child. The happiest person in the room was the baby of course. Both women left after Solomon made them sign up for an anatomy class at the local community college.

There are countless stories about Solomon involving his throne. On the steps of the throne, there were twelve golden lions, each facing a golden eagle. There were six steps to the throne, on which animals, all of gold, were arranged in the following order: on the first step a lion opposite an ox; on the second, a wolf opposite a sheep; on the third, a tiger opposite a camel; on the fourth, an eagle opposite a peacock, on the fifth, a cat opposite a cock; on the sixth, a sparrow-hawk opposite a dove. On the top of the throne was a dove holding a sparrow hawk in its claws, symbolizing the dominion of Israel over the Gentiles. Now I don't know about you, but this seems just a tad bit extravagant and gaudy. If I brought home a piece of furniture like that it would be relegated to the basement, and who would want to carry that to the basement? Hernias for everyone! This extravagance is a common theme throughout Solomon's rule. There was one point where he was poor and forced to be a cook. He did well with that, moving up to chef, then host, and then he owned the local T.G.I.F. in Israel. Before too long, he was back on the throne. Did all the wives waitress at the T.G.I.F? Hard to find evidence of that. His wealth was legendary. He was said to have amassed 39,000 plus pounds of gold in one year. Imagine the tax bill.

Solomon is most famous for building the temple in Jerusalem. The temple was designed by the people on HGTV. They wanted a log cabin with high ceilings and a lot of glass. Solomon looked at them and said "Have you looked outside? We've got like 3 trees in all of Jerusalem!" He quickly fired them and built the temple himself. Now with all the money he had amassed, they spared no expense. The temple was constructed sometime in the 10th century and destroyed 410 years later by King Nebuchadnezzar II.

That's a fun name to say. It is said to have housed the Ark of the Covenant. In case you forgot that's the vessel in which they kept the Ten Commandments, which were getting pretty dusty by then and needed a good cleaning.

There are no real descriptions of the size or look of the first temple, but I can imagine that it was more than impressive. Probably all stainless-steel kitchens, 100 bathrooms all with showers and whirlpools, rooms decorated by professionals for the temple priests, and I can't imagine how extravagant the room that housed the Ark of the Covenant was. Gold walls, wall-to-wall carpeting, a nice piped-in music system, and perfect lighting to highlight the ark's beauty. Of course, there were several outdoor swimming pools and lounging areas. Several wine bars and many types of fine wine. "Would you like a chateau blush wine sir? It's a 901 BC".

Just a guess but I'm probably not too far off. O.K. I'm probably way off. But the temple was built to be God's house. I'm sure they thought God deserved the best and spared no expense. Does God have a Saint of interior design? There's a patron saint for just about everything, so why not one for interior design? And maybe one for architecture. Anyhow, the house of God according to all accounts was quite a sight to behold. I just read that the temple had a porch. Maybe some nice rocking chairs for people to take a load off and relax before prayers. In the main area of the temple, animals were brought in for sacrifice. You name it, they killed it, except for the so-called "unclean animals." Lambs seemed to be the favorite and could be bought across the street at "Harry's House of

Lambs" on Grand Ave. Doves were also popular. I wonder how many lambs lost their lives over the years. And you would think God would be tired of eating lamb. The sacrifices had their throats slashed and then were thrown on a fire to offer their burning remains up to God. No mashed potatoes or gravy were ever sacrificed. And God must have not liked vegetables either.

The queen of Sheba was also associated with Solomon. It's a little confusing trying to figure out if they were friends or maybe a little bit more. Some accounts say he had a son with her who later became a king. Other accounts say they just played checkers and talked about the stock market while walking around the palace. I'm not sure which one it is, but I'm pretty sure he didn't make her wife number 701. The ancient limit was 700 and fines could be levied if more were taken.

Solomon, according to the Jewish bible, died of natural causes at the age of 80 probably because he wanted to. My Dad used to tell a joke that went like this. "Why do men die before women in a marriage? Because they want to." I miss dad's jokes. I think in this case he was right. After living with 700 wives and 300 concubines all complaining that you're working too late, and you never pay attention to them, he gladly checked out.

Next, we have Elijah. Elijah's story is also very confusing. The Bible is very vague on its origins. It is not known if he was a real man or an angel taking the form of a man. It appears that Elijah had a lot of problems with a woman named Jezebel. She threatened to kill him after he ordered the deaths of her priests. I can see her reasons for being so angry. You finally get a good bunch of priests you can trust and then they're gone. But then Elijah predicted Jezebel's death. Later, Elijah flees to Beersheba in Judah, continues alone into the wilderness, and finally sits down under a Retamaine shrub, praying for death. He falls asleep under the tree; an angel touches him and tells him to wake up and eat. When he awakens, he finds bread and a jar of water. He eats, drinks, and goes back to sleep. The angel comes a second time and tells him to eat and drink because he has a long journey ahead of him.

Elijah then takes a walk to Mount Horeb which again, going with the travel theme of the bible, takes 40 days and 40 nights. Why does everything take 40 days and 40 nights? Bad subway system? Can't get a flight out? Or is everything exactly 40 days and 40 nights away? I'm pretty sure at this point that nobody had a map. Elijah in so many words, has an argument with God in a cave on Mount Horeb. I'm thinking this is not a good thing to do. God will win every time. He knows all the angles in an argument because of the God thing, so Elijah should have quit when he was ahead. He is sent out again eventually where he runs into Jezebel who is his cat woman to his Batman. They have a problem with a vineyard that Jezebel and a friend took over by murdering its owner. Elijah's not happy and if I interpreted it right Jezebel is devoured by dogs.

Elijah eventually parts on a chariot of fire ascending to heaven in style. Now you decide if he was a man or an angel because I'm really confused.

Now let's skip ahead to by far the funniest name in

the Old Testament. Nebuchadnezzar II. This dude was ruthless. He took taking over countries to a whole new level capturing Jerusalem in 597 BC and deposing King Jehoiakim, then in 587 BC due to rebellion, destroying both the city and the temple, and deporting many of the prominent citizens along with a sizable portion of the Jewish population of Judea to Babylon. Not a nice guy at all. Although I'm sure he destroyed the temple, how do you burn a stone building down? I'll ask my brother, he's a fireman. Nebuchadnezzar is widely known through his portrayal in the Bible, especially the Book of Daniel. Daniel, who had been exiled to Babylon, becomes one of Nebuchadnezzar's favorite advisors for his interpretation of dreams and his ability to beat Nebuchadnezzar in monopoly. (Another day in purgatory. What am I up to now?) Nebuchadnezzar has a dream about a very large statue made of Gold, silver, bronze, iron and clay. He asks all his advisors what it means but Daniel is the only one who knows the answer. Nebuchadnezzar is representative of the golden head as a strong and great leader. Every part lower than that eventually gets weaker until the clay feet. This dream represents the eventual Babylon kingdoms after him getting weaker and weaker. All the people were forced to worship and bow down to this idol. Three Jewish men basically told Nebuchadnezzar to go to hell and didn't bow down to the idol. He was, to say the least a little aggravated and had them thrown into a furnace. As they were being led into the furnace Daniel and the three were praying to God to protect them. They were thrown into the furnace but must have been wearing flame-retardant suits because they didn't burn. An angel or God appeared behind them in the furnace to protect them and they walked out of the furnace with the ropes that bound them burned off but the three were not consumed at all by the fire. Not even the need for a Band-Aid. Nebuchadnezzar was amazed and thinking it was some party trick, stuck his hand in the fire only to be badly burned.

While boasting about his achievements, Nebuchadnezzar is humbled by God. The king loses his sanity and lives in the wild like an animal for seven years. After this, his sanity and position are restored, and he praises and honors God. Seems like a smart thing to do after all that. Nebuchadnezzar is one of the bigger parts of the Old Testament for a guy who was so ruthless to the Jewish people. It must have been pretty hard to assassinate a king back then because I would have taken a shot. Maybe I could get him to go to the theatre for a play? What too soon?

The story of Daniel in the lions' den is found in the sixth chapter of the Book of Daniel in the Hebrew Bible, and the lesser-known story of Bel and the Dragon in the Greek versions. Daniel is an official in the Persian Empire under King Darius. Darius (at the instigation of his other officials) had made a decree that no one was to offer prayer to any god or man except him for a period of thirty days. Daniel continued to pray as was his habit, knowing that praying would have him killed. For this action, Darius had him arrested and thrown into a lions' den. However, he was unharmed, and after he was released the following morning, the people who had cajoled the king into making the decree (for the sole purpose of getting at Daniel) were thrown into the lions' den themselves. That'll teach them to mess with Daniel. Daniel retired at this point and became a lion tamer in the circus. NO! Bad writer!

There are differing accounts about Daniel's age when he died. It seems like he was about 101 years old. If a lion can't get you, I guess most other things won't either. The question of how he died is still debated.

Jonah is the next figure in our story. It is one of the ones I have a hard time with and believe it is more of a fable than a true story. Jonah is told by God to go to the city of Nineveh because they're a rowdy bunch and out of control. Jonah doesn't want to go and disobeys God and heads in the opposite direction. He eventually gets on a boat with a bunch of sailors. A very large storm blows up and the sailors realize that Jonah has brought them bad luck and throw him overboard and the storm stops. Jonah is then swallowed by a large whale or fish (the bible's not too clear on this one) and has to stay in the belly of the beast for 3 days which is much better than the customary 40 days and 40 nights. Kind of a long weekend away. The whale spits Jonah out on a beach where he works on his tan for 40 days and 40 nights. Kidding. He returns to the city God wanted him to go to and they repent, and I do believe everything turns out o.k. Now I've been in the medical field for some 30 years and I've seen stomach acid at work. Jonah must have held on to the whale's uvula to prevent him from falling in the stomach. This would cause the whale to constantly try to clear his throat making all his other whale friends very annoyed with him. Sorry, this one is just too far-fetched for me.

The Old Testament was compiled and edited by various menover a period of centuries, with many scholars concluding that the Hebrew canon was solidified by about the 3rd century BC.

I found some of the really outdated rules from the Old Testament and found them pretty funny. They are as follows:

- "I permit no woman to teach or have authority over men; she is to keep silent." Timothy 2:11 Well this is going to set back the women's movement in a big way.
- "He that is wounded in the stones, or hath his privy member cut off, shall not enter into the congregation of the Lord."(Deuteronomy 23:1) Hold on, I have to go check myself.
- "But I say unto you, that whosoever looketh on a woman to lust after her hath committed adultery with her already in his heart." (Matthew 5:28) Boy I'm in big trouble and it's all Sandra Bullock's fault.
- "Whosoever putteth away his wife, and marrieth another, committeth adultery: and whosoever marrieth her that is put away from her husband committeth adultery." (Luke 16:18) If you're divorced and remarried, you're pretty much out.
- "A bitched shall not enter into the congregation of the Lord; even to his tenth generation shall he not enter into the congregation of the Lord." (Deuteronomy 23:2) Bitched means bastard in the bible. So, if

you don't know who your dad is, you can stay home on Sunday and watch football.

• "But every woman that prayeth or prophesieth with her head uncovered dishonoureth her head..." 1 Corinthians 11:5 No use showing off the new hairdo in church. Cover it up or you're in trouble.

• If in spite of this you still do not listen to me but continue to be hostile toward me, 28 then in my anger I will be hostile toward you, and I myself will punish you for your sins seven times over. 29 You will eat the flesh of your sons and the flesh of your daughters."(Leviticus 26:27-30) Eating babies? REALLY !

• "When men strive together one with another, and the wife of the one draweth near for to deliver her husband out of the hand of him that smiteth him, and putteth forth her hand, and taketh him by the secrets: Then thou shalt cut off her hand, thine eye shall not pity her." (Deuteronomy 25:11-12) So if you're in a fight with another guy and your wife grabs him by the private parts, she gets her hand cut off. Nice. Trying to help and look what happens.

• "But if this thing be true, and the tokens of virginity be not found for the damsel: Then they shall bring out the damsel to the door of her father's house, and the men of her city shall stone her with stones that she die: because she hath wrought folly in Israel, to play the whore in her father's house: so shalt thou put evil away from among you." (Deuteronomy 22: 20-21) All non-virgins step forward for your stoning.

- "For everyone that curseth his father or his mother shall be surely put to death: he hath cursed his father or his mother; his blood shall be upon him." (Leviticus 20:9) Sorry Mom and Dad.
- "But if she bear a maid child, then she shall be unclean two weeks, as in her separation: and she shall continue in the blood of her purifying threescore and six days." (Leviticus 12:5) If a woman gives birth to a daughter she is considered "unclean for 66 days".
- "Master, Moses wrote unto us, if a man's brother dies, and leave his wife behind him, and leave no children, that his brother should take his wife, and raise up seed unto his brother." (Mark 12:19) If your brother's wife is hot, you got it made.

The Old Testament reminds me of a father who is very strict with his children and sometimes even mean when they are growing up. As he ages, he starts to mellow and for this example let's say the New Testament represents his grandchildren. He has mellowed and become more loving and understanding of the mistakes made by human beings and forgives them for most of them. He just wants love and happiness. Now he still has his occasional outbursts, but nothing compared to what he did when he was a younger more Old Testament kind of Dad.

Several religions rely solely on the Old Testament for their laws and adhere to them pretty much to the letter. I'm not sure if that's the right thing to do. If we incorporate both Testaments into one bible that shows God can be compassionate too, the world might be a better place with less fighting and more understanding. Do I think one religion holds all the answers...NO.? Do I think we should do away with all religions...Maybe? Now that a bunch of you hate me let's move on to the New Testament.

The New Testament has a more loving, less angry God. He or she (threw it in there again just to make you think) seems to have mellowed and is much more occupied with the idea of us loving one another and being good people than blowing up cities and having to eat your babies. This is where I believe God shows his true colors. Maybe accepting us for our flaws and taking care of the evil people when they pass away. The New Testament has some things in it that still confuse me, but in general, I think it's a much more pleasant read.

I feel the need to give you some history that you may not know. Christian accounts in the New Testament are based a lot on oral traditions. The four canonical gospels are Mathew, Mark, Luke and John. When I say canonical gospels, I'm referring to the gospels that were approved to be a part of the New Testament. This occurred during the era of Constantine Emperor of Rome in the 300 A.D. era. There are many other gospels, they just didn't make the cut. So basically 300 years after Jesus's death the final version of the New Testament was complete. The earliest Gospel was written by Mark between 66-70 A.D. Most modern scholars reject the tradition which ascribes it to Mark the Evangelist, the companion of Peter, and regard it as the work of an unknown author working with various sources including collections of miracle stories, controversial stories, parables, and a passionate narrative. The Gospel of Matthew is generally believed to have been composed between 70 and 110 A.D., with most scholars preferring the period 80–90 A.D. Again, the true author is unknown but thought to be a well-educated Jewish man. The gospel of Luke, According to the preface, the purpose of Luke is to write an historical account, while bringing out the theological significance of the history. Most scholars say it was written sometime in the first century. Again, it is not agreed upon whether or not Luke actually wrote the Gospel or if it was authored by someone else. The Gospel according to John was written in its final form by 90 to 100 A.D. It is originally thought to be written by the apostle John or one of his close disciples. According to some, the Gospel of John developed over a period of time in various stages. Again no one is sure if the writer was truly John the Apostle but it may be a second or third-hand account from one of the disciples of John. All of this is very confusing to me now that I've researched it. As a kid, I was always under the impression that the gospels were written by the apostles. But when you look at the fact that most people were illiterate back then most of history was from the spoken word.

Now the hard thing for me to get past is the game we use to play in grade school. It was called the Chinese telephone. I don't know what it had to do with the Chinese, maybe they had a subpar phone system at the time, but the game went something like this. The teacher would line us up single file. She would whisper a sentence in the first person's ear, and they would have to turn around and whisper it into the next person's ear, and so on. By the time it got to the last person the sentence was completely or at least partially wrong. It was a real lesson in the fact that people not only hear what they want to but also add words to a statement if they are not sure what was said. I'm not saying that all the stories in the gospels are fabricated or based on half-truths, I just wonder if some of the facts got lost in the oral history. Jesus may have been responsible for even more miracles or even greater ones, but they could have been lost in the oral history. But saying that you have to also say that maybe some of the miracles were embellished like I embellished my weight (downward) on my driver's license. Ultimately, we'll never know what is perfectly written and what is not. The gospels themselves don't all agree on the facts and there are stories written in some that are omitted from others. Also, when the Dead Sea scrolls were found between 1946 to 1956, it added a whole new dimension to the possibilities. Also, other evidence of gospels found over the years suggests that there was a gospel of Mary, a gospel of Thomas, a gospel of truth, a gospel of Philip, and even a gospel of Judas, which I must say changes everything about the man who is thought to have betrayed Jesus. He may have not taken his own life; he may have continued to preach and was thought by some people to have been assigned the task of betrayal by Jesus himself. This seems very hard to believe, but again it's hard to know. Mary Magdalene was given the title of whore throughout the ages until someone realized it was probably not true and the church stopped referring to her as a whore. Each religion that follows the

New Testament has added its own rules and regulations causing more wars in the name of Christianity. We'll get into that later.

So, let's start with Mary the mother of Jesus. She is visited by an angel and is told that she will become pregnant with the son of God. Mary, obviously more than a little shocked, quickly reminds the angel that she is a virgin, and this isn't going to fly with her fiancé, not to mention the rest of the community. The angel tells her that all that will be taken care of, and Mary accepts the angel's words and becomes pregnant. Of course, being pregnant with the son of God you think would have its advantages. Maybe no morning sickness, knowing the pregnancy and birth will go well in a time that 50% of children born died before the age of two not to mention how many mothers died in childbirth. Knowing the virtues of Mary, she probably didn't go around bragging about carrying the son of God.

Now as you can imagine Mary has to tell Joseph, her fiancé, that she is pregnant and the fact that Joseph had never known Mary biblically as they say, he had a real problem with this. I mean when you think about it, if your fiancé told you she was pregnant with the son of God and you had never slept with her, her story would be a little hard to believe to say the least. Joseph shunned her in the beginning but was visited by an angel in a dream. The angel said, "Don't be afraid to take Mary as your wife" and being that dreams that include angels are usually a pretty reliable sign from God, Joseph went along with it. He protected Mary and went ahead with the wedding. Mary had the best tailor in Nazareth let out the wedding dress just enough, so she didn't show. (Another day in purgatory, I'm going to need a calculator soon to keep track of all of them). They were married in a nice ceremony with only one incident. Joseph's brother had a drinking problem and was dancing on the head table and unfortunately, stepped in the wedding cake ruining dessert for everyone. No one knows the brother's real name, but his nickname was "Party."

After the wedding, it was obvious that Mary needed a vacation. Mary visits her relative Elizabeth; they are both pregnant. Mary is pregnant with Jesus and Elizabeth is pregnant with John the Baptist. Now this is a very special family. Elizabeth was thought to be too old to conceive a child but God said, "I can do anything I want" and made it happen. It is thought that Joseph accompanied Mary to see Elizabeth but was quickly sent home because the ladies said they needed some "girl time" and went to the beach to work on their tans. John the Baptist is thought to have jumped in the womb when Mary arrived at Elizabeth's house.

Joseph went home but returned 3 months later (talk about an extended vacation) to retrieve Mary. Mary didn't want to go back because tanning lotion had just been invented and she was almost at a point where she thought her tan was "perfect". Joseph said, "I love you just the way you are" and then Billy Joel wrote a song about it. Alright, I skipped ahead a little.

According to the bible the Romans demanded a census be taken to make sure everyone was paying their taxes (sounds familiar). They told all the Jewish men that they had to return to their city of birth to be counted. There is no real evidence for this written anywhere in Roman history as a practice to evaluate the number of Jews. So maybe Joseph took Mary back to Bethlehem to visit his parents or to brag about his popularity in High School. Again, it's a mystery, and we don't know for sure why they went back to Bethlehem. Mary was in the last month of her pregnancy and had to travel on a donkey about a hundred miles to get to Bethlehem. As any of you know who have had kids the last thing you want to do with a woman who's eight months pregnant is take her on a long donkey ride through the wilderness to get anywhere. I'm not sure how the conversation went, but I'm thinking Mary was more than a little angry about the whole thing. She probably gave Joseph an earful and pulled the "Son of God" card quite a bit.

They eventually made it to Bethlehem and checked out all the hotels because the hospital was still under construction, so the doctors were all out playing golf. (No titanium drivers back then so the average drive was only 200 yards). They Joseph tried to check in at the Holiday Inn, The Marriott which had an indoor pool and free continental breakfast, the Embassy Suites, and even the raunchiest hotel in Bethlehem called "Abraham's Sleep and Creep Motel and Bar" but they were all booked. Seems there was an Amway convention in town and all the rooms were booked but the place was spotless due to the fine cleaning products Amway supplied.

They ended up at the Grand Hotel which was empty cold and bare but with the rolling truck stone thing just outside making our music there. Sorry, I just had a minor stroke and started quoting "Smoke on the Water" by Deep Purple. Actually, the only area available was a area referred to a "Guest room" or in some accounts just a cave. Jesus is born with the help of a midwife according to some of the History Channel shows and is placed in a manger. There are accounts of animals being in the room who all grow quiet while the birth is occurring. Within a short time, people started showing up. They wanted to see the Miracle baby that had been foretold. It is also thought that three wise men showed up with gifts of gold, frankincense, and myrrh. I understand the gold, the other two are a little confusing to me as gifts for a baby. You could put the gold in a bank as a college fund for Jesus. The other stuff is pretty much useless unless you're trying to freshen up a room. Now that I think about it that may be a good gift. With all those animals in there, it couldn't have smelled nice. So, all in all, the gifts were well thought out. After the visitors leave including the wise men, Mary gets some well-deserved rest and sleeps. Joseph can't find the pacifier and thinks of waking Mary, but after looking in the bottom of the diaper bag, he finds it and Jesus settles down for the night.

During the night while Joseph was sleeping, he had a dream that instructed him to get out of Bethlehem ASAP. Joseph quickly got Mary and the baby together and headed out even though Mary's HMO said she could stay for two days. They left the city and headed to Egypt to escape Herod's wrath. It is thought that the three kings stopped by to inform Herod that a new king of the Jews had been born in Bethlehem. Herod being the absolute jerk that he was had no intention of giving up his title to some new baby. So, he ordered what is referred to as the "Death of the Innocents". He decreed that any male child under the age of two in Bethlehem be killed. The order was carried out and Herod is also sitting next to Hitler in Hell because of it. Jesus, Mary and Joseph (I just had a flashback to my youth when my dad use to yell at me for not cutting the grass) got out of the city before Harrod's orders were carried out.

I should mention something about the star of Bethlehem. Many people have wondered what the star actually was. The wise man followed it from the east to an area just north of Jerusalem when it suddenly made a sharp left turn going south to Bethlehem where is stopped over the birthplace of Jesus. There was a show on H2 about the star and what it could have been. Comet, asteroid, meteorite, it goes on and on. If God really can make anything happen, he really impressed me with this one. I would imagine it's hard to move a star straight let alone make it take a hard left at a certain point and then stop. It was brighter than any other star in the sky so he had to up the wattage quite a bit too. All and all, some pretty impressive work. This is also one of those stories that is a little hard to believe for me. But again, who knows what really happened. Maybe a nova that occurred and eventually dimmed and disappeared from the sky. God made another Nova later, which was one of the worst cars I ever had.

Joseph led the family safely back to Nazareth where they resumed a normal life. Well as normal as can be expected being that you're now responsible for raising the Son of God.

John the Baptist was born about 6 months before Jesus and relentlessly teased him about being the oldest. Jesus, being the nice guy that he was took it in stride but occasionally put a little cod liver oil in John's milk just to get back at him. (Just a theory). John was kind a recluse living in the wilderness fasting and praying, fasting and praying. He didn't even go to his high school prom and was voted most likely to be a Saint someday. He was a beloved preacher and profit and had quite a large following. They opened a Starbucks near the river Jordan to accommodate all the people waiting to be baptized. It is still one of the most successful Starbucks franchises in the history of the company. John is said in many accounts from the bible to be the one that baptized Jesus It took place in the river Jordan according to some accounts. Again, the accounts mention several places and GPS was in its infancy mainly relying on the sun for location and the occasional statement from "OnStar" not associated with any of the other famous stars in the bible. According to several accounts, John was quite the preacher. He asked people to repent for their sins because the chosen one was already here. The kingdom of heaven would be theirs if they repented their sins. When Jesus did show up to be baptized John announced to the crowd that Jesus was the Son of Man and suggested to his disciples to follow him now. Several of John's disciples were angry because they had just bought houses along the river Jordan with boat docks and all the amenities and now John wanted them to follow Jesus.

Jesus needed to be alone for...You guessed it, 40 days and 40 nights of fasting and being tempted by the devil. Jesus resisted (you knew he would) and eventually reappeared and John's disciples joined him. They had gotten a good real estate agent who sold their houses in a month, and they went off with Jesus. This was the start of Jesus's ministry, and his father was pleased as stated in the bible.

Back to John the Baptist. Herod, the nasty and not well-liked Jewish king of Jerusalem as appointed by Rome, because at the time, Rome ran the show. John had confronted Herod about marrying his brother's wife and it made Herod's wife a little bit cranky. John, not one to pull any punches really let the two of them have it. This got him in big trouble not to mention the fact that he was amassing great crowds for baptism, and it was making the roman's nervous. John was eventually arrested and thrown in jail. Jail was usually a cave with some iron bars across the front. He was beaten severely and tortured. The romans were not a people who foreseen the Geneva Convention coming up. Eventually John was executed by removing his head (which is a vital part of the body if you want to contribute to society) and his head was presented to Herod and his wife. What did she ask for next? This woman has some serious mental issues that need to be addressed.

Back to Jesus. His life is filled with gaps of time. There is mention in the bible of Jesus being brought to the temple by Mary and Joseph 40 days (40 days again) after his birth to be blessed and I assume circumcised. Mary and Joseph were too poor to provide a lamb for sacrifice, so they had to settle for either two doves or two pigeons. I hope it was pigeons, I hate those things. One of the scholars was said to have prayed that he had finally seen the Messiah which was all he wanted before his death. I hope he didn't walk out of the temple and keel over. That's a little soon. Give him a couple of days to get his affairs in order. After the ceremony, Jesus, Mary, and Joseph end up in Egypt. Jesus walks around showing off to his friends by lifting the pyramids with his mind and walking across the Nile stepping only on crocodile's heads as he crosses. (How many days am I up to in purgatory? When I get to a year someone yells).

Actually, there is nothing written about Jesus's early life. Where he went to school, what kind of grades he got, whether or not he "Lettered in football, baseball, or soccer" (I'm betting soccer, they play a lot of that over there). After a short time in Egypt King Herod bites the dust and Joseph feels it's safe to go back to Nazareth. They take the 114 train out of Cairo which had several stops, which really annoyed Mary, until they got to Nazareth. Or they rode a donkey. I'm betting donkey, you just can't trust the internet for your information. Now this is one of the greater mysteries of the New Testament. The gaps in Jesus's life are many. The next time he's mentioned, he's roughly 12 years old and discussing the scriptures with the elders in the temple. This is mentioned only in Luke 2:41-52. Jesus had accompanied a Mary and Joseph and a large group of relatives and friends on a pilgrimage to Jerusalem. One the last day of the trip Jesus lingers in the temple and gets separated from Mary and Joseph.

They think he's with their entourage and they head back to Nazareth. After a day of travel, Mary realizes that Jesus is not with them, and she and Joseph call a cab and get back to Jerusalem to find the little whipper snapper. After three days of looking, they finally find him in the arcade playing Pac-Man and other games. Sorry. They find him in the temple He was found in the Temple in discussion with the elders who were amazed at his ability to quote scripture and interpret it. They quickly drafted him in the first round in exchange for two outfielders and a player to be named later. When Mary found him, she gave him a good talking to. Jesus said "Why do you seek me? Did you not know that I would be in my father's house"? Mary grounded him for two weeks and took away his TV privileges. Jesus went back to Nazareth with them and was given the silent treatment by both Mary and Joseph. Joseph thought about spanking him but decided spanking the son of God may be a big mistake in the big picture. What happened to the time before that happened? I want to know. Did he play Little League baseball? How about his behavior in school? I'm sure it was good being the son of God and all. In several places in the bible, it mentions that Jesus had 4 brothers (James, Joseph, Judes, and Simon) and an unknown amount of sisters. Again, another example of how little women were considered in ancient times. Let's say their names were Shaniqua and Edna. That's probably making the sisters mad in heaven, but someone's got to give them names. Why not me? Some say they were Joseph's kids from another marriage, some say they were his true brothers and sisters. The church wanted to maintain

Mary's complete and total virginity, so a lot of writings refer to Jesus's brothers and sisters being stepchildren for Mary. It was very common to have a big family back then because of the short life span of even children. Many died at early ages of things that we take a pill for or have a minor surgery for. Can you imagine how many children died of things like appendicitis? Even small infections could kill. It is thought that at least James was one of the apostles. Hard to say, James and the other names were pretty popular back then. So, it remains a mystery. Jesus referred to all his followers as his brothers and sisters so who knows? Any one of them could have been one of his brothers or sisters.

Jesus is thought to have started his ministry at the age of 30. So, what was he doing between the age of 12 and the age of 30? This is where things get very confusing for scholars and historians. It was extremely rare back then for a Jewish man to be single at any age over 18. Although a lot of them still lived with their mothers. Bad Joke. Bad Scotty. Could Jesus have had a wife in this time span or was he out in the wilderness waiting and praying for his time to come? Could he have had children? Did he have a job? Many of these questions may never be answered unless some new scrolls are found in the desert. This seems so against religious beliefs but if you look at it openly, Jesus may have had a wife that passed away before his ministry started. Maybe as many of them did she passed away during childbirth. We probably won't know until Jesus fills us in when we get to heaven. I'll probably be last in line, so you'll know before me. Maybe someone can sneak to the back of the line and fill me in. I can't wait to find out some of history's great mysteries.

Now Jesus's father/stepfather was referred to in many writings as a carpenter. However, in the biblical translations that have occurred over the years, they may have been confused with either a bricklayer or kind of a handyman. So, it is possible that Jesus was taught the family business and helped his father with it. Although Joseph kind of drops out of the biblical picture after the incident in the temple. So, we don't know if he died, and Mary was left a widow with all those kids or if he was just overlooked. Being that the average life span back then according to most historians was about 40 years, it is possible that Joseph died of natural causes at a young (at least to us) age. Jesus and his brothers would have to take over the business and take care of their mother after this. That was a tradition. The Bible never mentions anything about Mary having a second husband. So, let's not go there.

Let's say on the other hand that Jesus was aware of his fate and decided the best way to achieve what he was sent down here to do was to fast and pray in the wilderness for many years until he was ready to start his ministry. Where did he travel to? Was he nomadic or did he stay in one place maybe just outside of Nazareth? A nice bed and breakfast maybe. If you look at the time it takes to become a rabbi or priest today, he may have gotten his doctorate from the University of Nazareth in biblical studies. The university had a weak football team but an excellent soccer team destroying neighboring towns in every match. Jesus was the goaltender and as of now, nothing had ever gotten by him. He put up an invisible wall in front of the goal and had a perfect shutout record 4 years in a row until he went pro. (How many days am I up to now?) University of Nazareth is now an online school only and they no longer participate in sports. Jesus blew out a knee during his rookie season and had to retire. He went back and got his doctorate from there and before he knew it, he was standing before John the Baptist.

After Jesus was baptized and John the Baptist was arrested and eventually executed Jesus decided to move (A good idea on his part after the whole Baptist thing) to Galilee. Jesus goes to the sea of Galilee and meets two fishermen. They are brother's names Simon who is called Peter and Andrew. They are not having a lot of luck fishing and their nets are a mess. Jesus wants them to go out on the water again even though they had just gotten in from an unsuccessful fishing trip. Andrew talks Peter into it even though Peter thinks Jesus may have a screw loose. (One more day). They go out and Jesus summons the fish to their nets, and they win the Galilee fishing tournament by a great margin. Peter hoists the trophy and Jesus is happy for him. But as Peter settles back down in the boat Jesus says, "come with me and I'll make you fishers of Men". Peter is hesitant but Andrew knows a miracle when he sees one and quickly agrees. Jesus finally talks Peter into it and the first two followers of Jesus are ready to go. James and John who were in their dad's boat next to Peter and Andrew and decided they just couldn't work for their father anymore (he was kind of bossy) and they also decided to follow Jesus. Now we're up to four.

Now I'm not sure where this fits in the story but I find it fascinating. Jesus is asked by his mother to attend a wedding. This makes me believe that he wasn't married, and Mary was very proud of him and wanted to show him off to her friends. Jesus brought along some of his disciples. At the wedding dinner, the best man made a speech and complained that they had run out of wine. He called the father of the bride cheap, and it started a fight Jesus had to break up. Mary said to Jesus "You know being the son of God and all you think you can do something about the wine situation here"? Jesus, just a little bit upset with his mom reluctantly asks the waiters to fill the jugs up with water. He then in what is recorded as his first miracle changes the water into wine. Mary said, "See, I told you he could do it"! The party continued until the best man got too drunk and made a pass at the bride. The groom got mad and kissed the best man's wife and all hell broke loose. Jesus had to knock some heads together to get them all to settle down. By the way the wine was bottled and sold as a "Vintage Jesus" for many thousands of dollars later on in his ministry. No. Bad writer. Jesus left the wedding without having cake. He was not a fan of sweets. He was the only Jewish man in history with 6 pack abs. Sorry, I stole that from the Big Bang Theory television show. So, get mad at them, not Me.

Saint Nicodemus was a Pharisee and a member of the Sanhedrin. Who was played in my favorite movie regarding the life of Jesus (Jesus of Nazareth) by Sir Lawrence Olivier in the movie. I think Nicodemus would be proud that such a famous, brilliant actor like Sir Lawrence

Olivier played him. Being a member of the Sanhedrin, which was the governing body of the Jewish people in Jerusalem and the spiritual leader was corrupt and most of them were rich landowners who were interested in manly their own gain. My opinion, but otherwise why were they so wealthy? Nicodemus was one of them, but I have a feeling he didn't get along with the leader of the Sanhedrin at the time, a guy named Caiaphas. (A nasty man with a bad temper and obvious single-mindedness). Caiaphas didn't like Jesus mainly because he looked like a member of the Grateful Dead and went against many of the teachings and policies of the Sanhedrin. Caiaphas was bent on finding a way to get rid of Jesus, but Nicodemus went against him in the vote to have him arrested saying the Sanhedrin should look at the miracles performed by Jesus and maybe evaluate closer if he could truly be the Messiah. Caiaphas, thinking that Jesus was just another false profit trying to point the people away from the establishment refused to listen to Nicodemus even though Nicodemus not only made a good argument but also threatened Caiaphas with a lawsuit. Nicodemus had the famous lawyers Dewey, Cheatum, and Howe and they were on Nicodemus's speed dial.

I like Nicodemus. He wasn't afraid to buck the establishment. I'm sure the rest of the Sanhedrin made fun of him, called him a "Jesus Freak", and told him he couldn't use the swings on the playground. But Nicodemus stuck with Jesus all the way to the end. He was even there at the crucifixion. He is now considered a Saint and walks around heaven doing Saintly things like making beautiful fields of flowers, arranging for me to meet Sandra Bullock, and playing basketball with Jesus anytime Jesus wants to get a game together. Just a good guy.

Jesus Ministry has some interesting questions about when it started and how long it was. Jesus is thought to be born between 7-2 B.C. That goes against some of the classic teachings of the church, but it is an estimation. Scholars guess that his ministry started in 27-29 A.D. and ended in 30-36 A.D. with his death. Now as you could imagine, estimating dates in antiquity can be a real crap shoot. Archeological and written evidence from sources such as the bible are at best an educated guess. Technically, his ministry did not end with his death. The Apostles and who knows how many disciples went out in several different directions to preach his words. Jesus is known to have spoken to thousands of people at a time. Now I have some confusion regarding this. I'm 52. Sometimes my wife calls me from the kitchen when I'm in the living room. If I catch a quick snippet of her voice my first reaction is what? Did you say something? Now my house isn't huge. The distance between the kitchen and living room is approximately 20 feet. Now I'm curious. Did some of Jesus's apostles invent the first PA system or was Jesus just a very loud speaker? Maybe God sent down a PA system and after Jesus was done speaking, they may have had Karaoke. I hear Paul always won with his rendition of "Wanted Dead or Alive" by Bon Jovi. Peter in second singing "Smells like Teen Spirit" by Nirvana and Judas in third with his rendition of "Running with the Devil" by Van Halen. Judas was thinking about his future. A good time was had by all.

At one of these meetings where it's estimated that

maybe 5 thousand people and there wasn't enough food to feed the masses. This miracle is mentioned in all 4 gospels. They had two fish and 5 loaves of bread. At first one of the disciples offered to go down to the local McDonalds and by Happy Meals for everyone. Jesus, being a man of great intelligence but not a man of wealth nixed this idea worrying about the cost and the fact that the order would take forever to be prepared. He decided it was time for another one of his miracles and asked the apostles to bring the baskets they had with the two fish and the loaf of bread in them out to the crowd. Within seconds the baskets were full and magically kept refilling themselves with fish and loaves until the whole crowd had their fill. Thomas kept looking at the bottom of the baskets thinking there was someone under there adding fish and bread to the baskets as they got low. Another reason they called him "Doubting Thomas". Always looking for the magic trick. Jesus gave him the "Look" and Thomas got the hint. There is a second miracle almost of the same magnitude where Jesus feeds 4,000 people with 7 loaves and a few small fish. This one is mentioned in Mark and Mathew's gospels but not in Luke and John because they were vacationing in the south of France where the wine tastings were very fancy. They had to get approval from Jesus for their vacation. Being the old softy that he is, he let them go only asking him to bring back a few bottles for the group. Luke and John said, "What's a bottle" and Jesus said, "Oh I forgot I haven't invented that yet". Bring back a couple of ceramic jars instead. Luke and John agreed and off they went much to the chagrin of the other apostles who hadn't had a vacation in over a year.

Jesus is credited with many miracles. Some of them involve cures and exorcisms, raising the dead, and controlling nature. If you put all of that in perspective, it's a pretty impressive resume'.

Now in my opinion and I don't think I'd get much of an argument from people, the most famous miracle is the raising of Lazarus from the dead. Lazarus had been dead for 4 days when Jesus was summoned by his sister Martha. By the time Jesus made it to Lazarus, he was more than dead. I've worked in the medical field for 30 years. The decaying of a body occurs almost immediately after death. There are live bacteria in the intestinal tract that start to feast on the host's tissue after the death. This causes ugly things to happen and a stench that will clear a room faster than a 2-year-old with a full diaper.

Jesus, being very confident and having the "Big Guy" on his side went down to the grave of Lazarus and prayed for God's intervention. Even though God was playing Golf and was about to sink a 40-foot putt (you know he'll sink it) he helped Jesus out. Jesus thanked him and stood up and called in a loud voice "Lazarus, come out"! And low and behold Lazarus walks out of the tomb still dressed in his burial clothing (white, not really Lazarus's color) and the crowd went wilder than the first audience at a Beatles concert here in the States. Jesus told Lazarus to "Take off your burial clothes and get into something more comfortable" and Jesus left. He wasn't one to stick around and gloat about his miracles. Very humble man that Jesus.

Lazarus went on to open the first Starbucks in his town and sold Jesus cups to all his customers. Whenever Jesus was back in town Lazarus would fix him the best Latte' he ever had in his life. (More time in purgatory. Who's keeping count out there)?

He also did the same for the daughter of Jairus. Jairus asked Jesus to heal his daughter. She was dying by the time Jairus reached Jesus. They couldn't get a cab and had to walk to Jairus's house. By the time they arrived, the little girl had already passed away. Jesus said, "She is not dead. Only sleeping". This angered the doctors who already had big egos back then. A tradition that continues today. Jesus walked right passed them into the little girl's tomb and told her to rise. He carried her out into the crowd and stood her up next to her father who hugged her and thanked Jesus for bringing her back. The doctors blamed it on faulty stethoscopes and charged Jairus anyway. Jesus didn't even leave a bill. He just went on his way.

I think in the overall picture of the New Testament the ability for Jesus to bring people back from the dead makes him more than a profit. There is something special about this man, and the way Christianity has grown over the last 2000 years I say most people believe he was the Christ. By the way, Christ is not Jesus's real last name. And a note to all my friends who like to bring up his name in frustrating situations, Jesus did not have a middle name or even use an initial. I remember the days of my father slamming his thumb with a hammer and yelling "Jesus H. Christ". Even though we know that he didn't have a middle name, what would the "H" have stood for? Herbert? Harry? Howard?

The possibilities are endless. My Dad knows now what if any middle name there is, God rest his soul.

Now all the other miracles are very impressive too. Walking on water (at my weight, just forget it), curing the blind, curing a leper, making my children believe I was the best hockey player that ever lived, all great miracles. Hey did you hear about the hockey game in the leper colony? There was a faceoff in the corner! Another bad joke courtesy of my father. He had a ton of them.

I always wanted to know more about the Twelve Apostles. We know about the main ones who wrote or are credited with the gospels but what about the others? Let's get into this.

The apostles were:

1. Simon who he later named Peter.
2. Andrew his brother
3. James
4. John (Also his brother)
5. Philip
6. Bartholomew
7. Thomas
8. Mathew (the tax collector) who was also named Levi (No he didn't invent the Jeans)
9. James the son of Alphaeus
10. Thaddaeus
11. Simon the Zealot
12. Judas Iscariot (still considered an apostle, although the end didn't go well for him) Judas was replaced by Matthias and a player to be named later.

Later the Catholic Church added many other "Apostles or Disciples" as they are called. They were pioneering Missionaries to many far-off lands who helped spread Christianity throughout the world.

One not mentioned is Mary Magdalene who was referred to in some texts as the "Apostle to the Apostles". She was one of Jesus's closest followers and for years was thought to be a repentant whore. A title that was given to her in medieval times when women were still frowned upon as leaders in the church. (Not that the Catholic Church has changed that much since that time, Women are still not allowed to be priests) The title was later removed and her role before her time with Jesus is speculated on to this day. The Novel "The Da Vinci Code" is loosely based on the book "Holy Blood Holy Grail" which puts Mary Magdalene in an entirely different light as the wife and mother of Jesus's daughter "Sara". The story is intriguing and if you haven't read the book or seen the movie, I would recommend it. Even though it's based on a novel, many facts about Mary are brought to light that may change her role in early Christianity. I'll let you decide. Don't close yourself off to the idea. Watch the movie. Tom Hanks is fantastic in it.

So, let's cover the apostles in a short synopsis of their lives.

Simon/Peter after Jesus's death ended up in Rome of all places teaching Christianity to the same people who put Jesus to death. Not a good career move in my opinion. It's kind of like walking around as a lamb in a lion pit. But Peter pressed on and was later elected the first Pope of the Roman Catholic Church. Peter appears to have lived a long life, but it did end in martyrdom. He was crucified on a cross but felt he wasn't worthy of the same death. He asked to be crucified upside down instead. You know I've got to say these Romans were real bastards. They thought of so many sick ways to kill a person it is unreal. All to prove their superiority in the world. Feeding people to the lions, having gladiators cut them up, setting them on fire, and making them watch reruns of "Full House". It's all so cruel. I'm sure so many of them are rotting in hell it's got its own section for them alone. Even though it is said that Jesus uttered the phrase "Forgive them, Father, for they know not what they do" I'm not sure that was enough to pacify God's wrath when they were brought over to the other side if you know what I mean. Peter was called the "Rock" because of his great wrestling skills and later starred in movies. What? Wrong Rock? He is said to be buried in Rome under the Basilica of Saint Peter. Although other sites are also claiming his bones.

Andrew was Simon/Peter's brother. They were both fishermen. Andrew was also a disciple of John the Baptist who would later tell him to follow Jesus. He preached along the black sea up as far as the Ukraine and maybe even into Russia. He was also martyred later in life on what's called an "X-shaped cross". He was bound to it but not nailed. Several experiments have been done to figure out what kills someone when they are crucified. It appears that the lungs can no longer inflate after a while, and you suffocate. Not exactly an easy way to go. Andrew is the patron saint of Ukraine, Romania, and Russia. He had nothing to do with the Cold War.

James the son of Zebedee was also the brother of John the Apostle. He is described as one of the first apostles to join Jesus. He is also believed to be the first apostle martyred. He went to Spain to preach. St. James returned to Judea, where he was beheaded (another favorite hobby of the Romans) by King Herod Agrippa I in the year 44 A.D.

John is the only apostle except for Judas Iscariot how was not martyred. It is thought that he may have truly written his gospel although there are many different opinions on this. He lived long enough to be responsible for it, but again, because it was so long ago, no one knows for sure. I like to think he did. It would make him the most important figure responsible for the details of Jesus's ministry. John was also the only apostle present at the crucifixion. John's racking up points right and left in my book. John went to Greece to preach and was later banished to an island of the coast of Greece where he finished out his days writing. Some say he wrote Revelation, another part of the bible. He was said to be the youngest of the apostles and to have lived longer than any of the others. They think he died in 98 A.D.

Philip the Apostle after the resurrection preached in Greece and Syria. He is reported to have performed his own miracles. He is mentioned in the Gospel of John most frequently. Philip was also crucified (this seems to be an ongoing them with these Romans) on the cross upside down after being tortured. He continued to preach from the cross until he died. On Wednesday, 27 July 2011, the

Turkish news agency Anadolu reported that archeologists had unearthed a tomb that the project leader claims to be the Tomb of Saint Philip during excavations in Hierapolis close to the Turkish city Denizli. The Italian archaeologist, Professor Francesco D'Andria stated that scientists had discovered the tomb within a newly revealed church. He stated that the design of the Tomb, and writings on its walls, definitively prove it belonged to the martyred Apostle of Jesus. After all these years, it's amazing to me that such a tomb can still be discovered. Everyone out there keep digging. You never know what you'll find.

http://en.wikipedia.org/wiki/Philip_the_Apostle

Bartholomew is the next apostle we'll look at. He seems to be the least know of the apostles. Obviously didn't have a good PR man. Bartholomew was thought to be brought into the inner circle by Philip the Apostle. They owned a company called "Donkeys R Us" and decided that the business wasn't worth the trouble, and both decided to follow Jesus. After the ascension of Jesus, he is thought to have made a pilgrimage to India to preach. He also traveled to Ethiopia and Armenia. He is one of the patron saints in Armenia and is credited with at least two miracles in Armenia. There is conflict as to how Bartholomew was martyred. In one account he was beheaded. In the other account he was flayed and then crucified. Flayed is the removal of one's skin while they are still alive. Who thinks of these things? Sick bastards. There is one painting of Bartholomew holding his own skin while being crucified upside-down on the cross. This all happened in Armenia. It's pretty amazing to me how these martyred Apostles always end up being the patron saint of the country that crucified them. You think they would ask God for another country where they were treated better.

http://en.wikipedia.org/wiki/Bartholomew_the_Apostle

The apostle Thomas

Also referred to as "Doubting Thomas" because of his disbelief of the resurrection of Jesus. Jesus appeared to all of the apostles and asked Thomas to feel the holes in his hands and the wound from a lance on his side. This convinced Thomas (as it should of) that Jesus had risen from the dead. After Jesus left (had to catch a flight to London where the ancestors of the Clash were playing, Jesus is a big Clash fan) Thomas went off to India to preach. According to The Passing of Mary, a text attributed to Joseph of Arimathaea, Thomas was the only witness of the Assumption of Mary into heaven. We all assume that by saying "Mary" he meant Jesus's mother. There are more Mary's mentioned in the bible than any other female name. It was the most popular name back then so there was a lot of mix ups with lunch boxes at school.

There is some controversy about Thomas's death. Several accounts say he was martyred by being stabbed by 4 soldiers, but other accounts say he died of natural causes. Again, it's hard to tell what account to believe. Most people believe he was martyred, but that may be because it makes the story a little more exciting. I like to think he died of natural causes because that would have allowed him to preach longer. Thomas also is said to have written a "Gospel" although it is considered one of the Gnostic gospels and wasn't included in the New Testament. It never mentions Jesus's crucifixion or resurrection. It is mainly filled with sayings attributed to Jesus. Sayings like "look both ways before you cross the street" and "A rolling stone gathers no moss". O.K. maybe those aren't in there but there are many others. Thomas seems to be an apostle who leaned more toward the idea that Jesus was a profit more than anything else. His constant doubting of Jesus's miracles and resurrection suggests that Thomas was a scholarly man who needed hard proof of everything. I'm not saying this is good or bad, but Jesus had a soft spot for those who believed without seeing, so you got to believe Thomas was not on Jesus's top ten list.

The Apostle Mathew

Here's an interesting story. First off, Mathew's real name was Levi. He invented button down jeans and made millions. Jesus refused to wear them because he said they "itched". (all these days in purgatory, what a shame). Levi's name was changed to Mathew not long after he joined Jesus. Now Mathew was not a shining star in the Israelite world. He was a tax collector for Herod Antipas and collected taxes from people like Peter on the fish he caught. Being a tax collector back them was a lot like being one now. You aren't going to have a big fan base. Matthew was hated by Peter not to mention several of the other apostles but was welcomed by Jesus because he knew showing that it is possible to love your enemies and make them understand that the mission was more important than anything else, he convinced Mathew and Peter to become best friends (at least in the beginning) and before long they were golf partners and would often play a round or two with Jesus's and Thomas who doubted the length of every drive Jesus had. Jesus would say "that looks like it was about three hundred yards"! And Thomas would say "it's only two fifty". Then Jesus would make Thomas miss his ball on the first swing and all the other apostles would laugh at him. Peter and Mathew would always let Jesus and Thomas win, because that's what you do when you play the boss in golf.

Mathew is one of the apostles that is said to be a witness to the resurrection and ascension of Jesus. Some people believe that Mathew wrote his gospel and others attribute it to an anonymous writer. He is said to have preached in Judea and other countries, but the countries are not mentioned. I'm guessing the United States wasn't an option because it was hard to get a passport back than to an undiscovered place.

Mathew was martyred by the sword. That's all that is written about it. There is one account of him dying of old age, but it is not a popular view. It is also said that Mathew and Peter didn't get along too well after they began their teachings. Something about Peter lying about a putt he made that Mathew said was technically a chip shot. It just escalated from there.

The Apostle James, Son of Alphaeus

James, son of Alphaeus, appears only four times in the New Testament, each time in a list of the twelve apostles. It is written that he was the brother of either Jesus, the cousin of Jesus, or the brother of one of the other apostles. Lots of differing accounts. There are so many

James references in the New Testament that it's hard to tell who's who. James son of Alphaeus seems to get lost in the mass. There isn't much written about him, although we know that Saint James was arrested along with an unspecified number of Christians and was subsequently beheaded by Herod in persecution of the church. Although there is one other story that confused me so much, I'm not even going to go into it. This one states that he was crucified in Egypt for preaching the gospel. Either way, as usual, things didn't end well for this apostle either.

Jude (Thaddeus) the Apostle

First off, they make it abundantly clear that Judas and Jude were two different people Jude was obviously better because the Beatles wrote a song about him. There is some question as to which Jude is the brother of Jesus. Again, the word "Brother" was thrown around like a Frisbee back then so were not sure if it meant cousin or actual brother. Thaddeus is thought to be a nickname (lousy nickname, how about Mack or Tiny instead) to discriminate between the Judas who betrayed Jesus and Jude.

According to tradition, Saint Jude suffered martyrdom about 65 AD in Beirut, in the Roman province of Syria, together with the apostle Simon the Zealot, with whom he is usually connected. Jude is thought to have been hanged.

The Apostle Simon the Zealot

This one is tough. Little is known about Simon the Zealot. It is said he preached in Egypt and many other places. Zealot is usually associated with someone who has great passion for his or her cause and is willing to even cause uprising against their oppressors. The romans spent many years crushing the zealot uprisings in Jesus's time. Because we know so little about Simon the Zealot all we can truly say is he probably was a zealot who started to follow Jesus.

There are several differing accounts of his death. Crucifixion, peaceful death, sawn in half, and made to watch the Tella Tubbies until he died. I think the latter would be the worst. Although sawn in half would be now picnic either. Simon the Zealot seems to be one of the mystery apostles that gets overlooked in a lot of history. His role at the time was unknown. But if he is said to be an apostle, I'm sure he worked as hard as the others in preaching the words of Jesus. I still can't get past the sawn in half thing.

Judas Iscariot

According to Roman Catholics Judas lost his status as an apostle when he supposedly betrayed Jesus. The reason I say supposedly is because in some writings, it is thought that Judas was one of Jesus's most trusted apostles and would be the only one who would be willing to set in motion the crucifixion and resurrection of Jesus. Jesus told him according to some accounts that his name would be scorned for eternity. He was still willing to do what Jesus asked him too even though it would paint him as the bad guy. I'm not sure what to believe. Someone had to set the whole process in motion to achieve salvation for all of God's people. Judas may have just "took one for the team". Gnostic texts actually praise Judas for his role in triggering humanity's alleged salvation, and view Judas as the best of the apostles. Furthermore, the Roman Catholic Church has never officially stated that it believes Judas is in Hell for his actions. So, if he did what he was told by Jesus, the hatred of Judas may be unfounded.

The traditional texts say that Judas betrayed Jesus for 30 pieces of silver and a red corvette. The corvette was filled with gas at the time but sat idle after Judas ran out. No gas stations (even self-serve) were around back then, and no one knew the concept of refining oil into gas. So, after a few spins around the city Judas started to feel guilty and it got the better of him. He was going to crash the corvette into a wall going about 90 mph to do himself in, but he just couldn't ruin such a fine automobile. He opted for hanging himself just outside the city. The 30 pieces of silver were found at his feet. The corvette is in the Jerusalem Museum but it is rarely brought out to show the people. It's kind of a public embarrassment. Alright, I took that way too far. I just had a visual of Judas whipping that vet around and showing off to all the ladies. You probably wouldn't want to be in my head most of the time. Judas's place in the group was replaced by Mathias.

Mathias (Lucky number 13) the Apostle

Mathias is the only apostle who was not chosen by Jesus. Jesus had already ascended to heaven when Mathias was drafted. He was a first-round pic because of his great throwing arm and his ability to scramble in the pocket.

There is no mention of a Matthias among the lists of disciples or followers of Jesus in the three synoptic gospels. According to *Acts* 1, in the days following the Ascension of Jesus, to the assembled disciples, who numbered about one hundred and twenty, that they nominated two men to replace Judas: Joseph called Barsabbas (also known as

Justus) and Matthias. Then they prayed, "Lord, you know everyone's heart. Show us which of these two you have chosen to take over this apostolic ministry, which Judas left to go where he belongs." Then they cast lots, and the lot fell to Matthias; so, he was added to the eleven apostles. He preached in Judea and a few other places and was eventually stoned to death for his preaching's. You know, I'm beginning to think that hanging around with Jesus in the early days was a definite death sentence.

http://en.wikipedia.org/wiki/Saint_Matthias

There you have it. The 12 apostles in a nutshell. There are many things I skipped, like some of the miracles that were attributed to them and all the places they traveled to preach. I've got to admire the tenacity that it took to go preach about a guy that a lot of people thought was another false profit. The number of profits (real or false) that were crucified in all parts of the Roman world is amazing. So just saying you believed in one wholeheartedly put you at great risk.

The mention of over 120 disciples in the previous paragraph makes the spread of the words and acts of Jesus more likely than just having 12 people talking about Jesus. It's like one of those pyramid schemes. Let's say each disciple or Apostle talks to a group of 20 people in a town. He gets a couple of them to follow him. After receiving their bachelor's degree in Jesus, they go off on their own and pick up disciples of their own. Before you know it, there are thousands of followers if not more. The Romans tried to suppress the movement as much as they could but by the 300's A.D. the Roman Emperor Constantine had a vision of the cross talking to him (which must have looked pretty funny) telling him he would win the upcoming battle. After that, he became an avid Christian and told everyone in Rome they had to do the same. Christianity became the state religion of Rome. How things change in a couple hundred years. The Christians went from being fed to the lions to running the show.

Well, I kind of got off track again. I'm trying to follow some sort of order but like my mind, this book will probably be all over the place. I hope you don't mind. And by now most of you who are very religious are looking up my address and calling your local mob contact to put out a contract on me. Please remember this is a lighthearted book on something that is not very lighthearted. But I think God has a sense of humor, at least I hope so.

So, let's get back to some of the miracles of Jesus. I already told you about Lazarus, which is thought to be Jesus's last miracle (other than the whole raising himself from the dead thing). The miracles of Jesus are the supernatural deeds attributed to Jesus in Christian texts. According to the Gospel of John, only some of these were recorded. They have been categorized by Henrik Van der Loos into four groups: cures, exorcisms, the resurrection of the dead, and control over nature. http://en.wikipedia.org/wiki/Miracles_of_Jesus Although all of them are very interesting I find the healing of the lepers most intriguing. Again, I have worked in the medical field for a long time. I've never seen a leper, but I've been told it's not a disease you want. Globally in 2012 the amount of people who had leprosy was about 180,000. It is now a curable disease that is mainly caused by one or two infections. It can cause numbness and disfigured skin; the infections can eventually cause gangrene causing parts to fall off. Back then the only cure for leprosy was Jesus. If you were one of the few he healed in his ministry, you were lucky. The disease can last from 5 to 20 years.

In the Torah (also included within the Christian Old Testament), there are references to Moses and his sister Miriam being afflicted by a dreaded skin disease transliterated as tzaraath, which is widely but not exclusively understood to mean leprosy.

Jesus would lay his hands on the lepers, and they would magically be cured. This was frowned upon because lepers were thought to be "Unclean" and it was also thought the disease was transmitted by touch. It is rarely contagious, but in some cases, it can be transmitted from the respiratory tract. Jesus's cure was much more effective than the 6 to 12 months of medicine lepers have to go through to get cured nowadays. If you were a witness to such a healing by Jesus, you had to be impressed. That would get me to follow him, although my wife would probably be a little angry about me up and leaving her with 4 kids and a mortgage. That's another thing. How many of the Apostles left women and children behind to follow Jesus and did they send child support and alimony back to them in those days? Maybe Jesus felt guilty and wrote the checks. I'm sure he could fill his bank account at any time, and he need these men to help with his ministry. I'm sure he felt sorry for the women left behind. Although the mail was very slow (donkey delivery) they must have gotten checks to help support the family. (One more day in purgatory, but who's counting).

Now an exorcism I would think Jesus would need some help from his dad. Getting evil spirits (if you believe in such things) out of people is not easy. My sister had evil spirits in her when she was a teenager and my Dad tried to get them out but had little luck. They eventually went away on their own when she got married. Now she's a great lady and rarely is possessed by evil spirits. It only happens when her boys won't clean their room.

A large number of exorcisms are attributed to mental illness. Up until the 1800's mental illness was not understood. Medications for it were not very effective until the 1900's. Something as serious as schizophrenia or bipolar depression must have been looked upon as demons possessing a body back in Jesus's time. That doesn't mean that Jesus's didn't exorcise demons from people. I just wonder if some of the people he "Exorcised" were actually mentally ill. This is still a very impressive feat. Mental illness is still a mystery now days. Jesus's ability to heal at any level is impressive. Whether he was casting out the devil or somehow curing a severe mental illness is irrelevant in the scheme of things. Either way, it is a very impressive way of getting a crowd to believe in you as the Son of God.

Now the resurrection of the dead is by far a real crowd pleaser. I like the story of the little girl that Jesus resurrected more than anything. Because childhood death was so common back then pulling a child out of the depths of death would have gotten me on the Jesus bandwagon pretty quickly. I'm an old softy when it comes to kids. I've worked with them in the medical field for so many years now and I find that they still bring a smile to my face. The little girl was pronounced dead by the local doctor (which didn't require a degree, internship, or residency) while his father was asking Jesus to come and heal her. By the time Jesus arrived, the girl was already dead. Jesus said, "She is only sleeping" and went into the room where she was, and before you knew it, out comes Jesus holding the little girl. He stands her up and she is embraced by her parents. The doctor is sued for malpractice and the family settles out of court for 3 donkeys and 12 chickens. A pretty high price in those days. The doctor continues to practice, but anytime he pronounces anyone dead, people look at him funny and wait a couple of days before they go ahead and bury the body. Just being sure, I guess. Nowadays, the malpractice suit would have been settled and the family would be living in a new home on the lake with servants and a 4-car garage with sports cars filling all of them. The girl's college would be paid for and the father would be wearing a Rolex. As you can tell, I think malpractice suits have gotten a little out of hand.

The Control Over Nature

Jesus had a real talent for settling things down. If he was out with Peter and Andrew doing a little fishing and a storm blew in Jesus could just stand up in the boat, wave his arms, and the storm would disappear. Jesus would sit back down in his chase lounge and continue fishing. He liked fishing. It was very relaxing for him. And anytime Peter bragged about catching a 3-pound largemouth bass,

Jesus would pull up a 4-pounder just so Peter didn't get too big for his britches.

Jesus also had the ability to walk on water. Now back then morbid obesity was not a global problem so we can assume Jesus was a thin man. But still, walking across water is even harder for the best illusionists to do. Jesus made it look so easy. One time, Peter gave it a try and was doing very well until he started to doubt his abilities and not have faith in Jesus's ability to make Peter walk across water. Peter fell in ruining his best outfit and his Cell Phone. This was a real problem back then because the nearest AT&T store was many miles away and Peter didn't have the replacement insurance on the phone. Jesus decided to help him out and waved his hand over the cell phone and it was automatically dry, and Peter rejoiced. This miracle is hard to find in the bible. It's probably been left out over the years because AT&T sued for mentioning their name without permission. Oh no. That means I'm going to get sued too. Jesus's ability to control nature is an amazing feat in itself because after 2000 years we can't find a weatherman who can predict the weather accurately let alone control it.

The Sermon on the Mount

The teachings of the Sermon on the Mount have been a key element of Christian ethics, and for centuries the sermon has acted as a fundamental recipe for the conduct of the followers of Jesus. It is basically the rules and regulations given by Jesus early in his ministry. The sermon is the longest piece of teaching by Jesus in the New Testament. The lord's prayer is in the teaching along with many of his other "Hits". It occupies chapters 5, 6, and 7 of the gospels of Mathew. The sermon is one of the most widely quoted parts of the canonical gospels. The mount itself is never mentioned. The mount is very angry about being left out. It thinks geography is important and should receive more attention in the bible. The mount is a little bitter.

There is another story about the Centurion's servant. I like this one because it shows at least one of the Roman soldiers had a soft spot for Jesus. He was a believer even though it was forbidden. He had a servant who had been with him a long time. He thought of him as a son more than a servant. The centurion approached Jesus scattering the crowd with his presence. He told Jesus that the servant he thought of as a son was very sick and thought he would die unless Jesus intervened. The amazing thing about this story is that Jesus offered to go see the servant but the centurion said that he knew that Jesus had the power to heal by just saying the words. He knew that if Jesus said the servant would be healed, it would happen. He had such faith in him that he knew just saying it would make it happen. Jesus was so impressed with the man's faith he pointed it out to the whole crowd. His faith was greater than most. He believed Jesus would heal him and he did. By the time the centurion returned home the servant was healed and immediately borrowed his segregate Dads horse and went around the city whooping it up. He was immediately grounded for two weeks and made to write "I will not steal Dad's horse" 500 times. Blind faith always impressed Jesus.

Parable of the Mustard Seed

The parable of the Mustard Seed goes like this according to Mathew. He set another parable before them, saying, "The Kingdom of Heaven is like a grain of mustard seed, which a man took, and sowed in his field, which indeed is smaller than all seeds. But when it is grown, it is greater than the herbs, and becomes a tree, so that the birds of the air come and lodge in its branches." Now Jesus was calling it here. The kingdom he is said to be referring to is now the biggest religion on earth. Christianity has become number one. Using this parable, I think Jesus is referring to himself as the mustard seed and its growth being a representation of how his name and legend would grow over the years. We all know Jesus knew how to tell a story and he obviously could predict the future too. He could easily work for the psychic network. I know, I know. I'm in trouble for that one too.

Jesus and Children

Jesus said, "Let the little children come to me, and do not hinder them, for the kingdom of heaven belongs to such as these." This is one of my favorite sayings in Matthew's Gospel (Matthew 19:14). Children in my book are more than special. They are what makes a good deal of the happiness in the world. Even the ones that give you trouble are still cute as can be when they're trying to explain how the vase got broken. Jesus appears to have a soft spot in his heart for kids. He often would gather them around and talk to them at their level. Something all of us could learn from. He played video games with them (although he frowned upon Halo) and often taught them how to ride bikes and play baseball. He also wasn't afraid to show his feminine side by dressing up for the occasional "Tea Party" one of the little girls had planned. O.K. I'm not sure about that last one. But couldn't you see Jesus doing something like that just to make a little girl smile? Children are a big part of having a complete life in my book. I know some people are unable to have them. I think adoption is one of the most wonderful things one human can do for another. Giving a child a stable environment to grow up in and loving them like they are your own because they are. Sorry for the philosophy lesson, I'm a big teddy bear when it comes to kids. Somehow, I think when I cross over to the other side I'll be working with children because it's something I enjoy, and I think I'm pretty good at it. I have the "goofiness" gene. I'll do anything to make a child laugh. Nothing makes me happier. So, the fact that Jesus feels the same way makes me think he was a very special man. Not everyone has that skill. You don't have to look far to see that.

The rich young ruler

So, this rich dude approaches Jesus and asks him how he can get to heaven. Jesus looks at him and gives him some advice.

"If you want to be perfect, go, sell your possessions and give to the poor, and you will have treasure in heaven. Then come, follow me".

When he heard this, he became very sad, because he was a man of great wealth. Jesus looked at him and said, "How hard it is for the rich to enter the Kingdom of God

Indeed, it is easier for a camel to go through the eye of a needle than for a rich man to enter the kingdom of God."

Now this one is a little outdated. Most of the rich men back then were bent on keeping the wealth for themselves. Not that we don't have our fair share of that going on today. Can you say Enron? I knew you could. But I look at people like Bill Gates and Oprah Winfrey. They give Millions away to the poor and do things that benefit society greatly. Without Bill Gates, I'd be typing this on an old fashion typewriter using enough whiteout to make myself high as a kite. Bill Gates and Steve Jobs changed the world for the better with their inventions and abilities. I think God would be impressed. They have a lot of money but they're not afraid to give some of it away. Bill Gates puts computers in schools constantly. Steve Jobs is up in Heaven trying to explain his operating system to Jesus who is used to using a Windows-based product. Jesus is doing well, but he still likes to double-click on things.

Now a camel through the eye of a needle would take some serious work. If you are a rich man who is stingy with your money you are going to have to grind up that camel into very small pieces. Pushing them through the eye of a needle will take time. And then there is the problem of reassembling the camel after you're done because you know Jesus will want that done too just to prove his point. If I were a rich man, I would start giving away some money ASAP. The whole camel through the needle thing is a messy, daunting task.

The parable of the Ten Virgins

This doesn't relate to today. No one can find ten virgins.

There are many more parables I have left out or could not find a way to explain them to all of you. (Assuming more than one person reads this book). Although would like to give you one more based solely on my recognition for it from bible school when I was a kid.

A man had two sons. They both worked in the field very hard for him. One day the youngest son came up to his father and said, "Give me my inheritance now so I may go out on my own and explore the world". (Paraphrasing). So, the man did, and the son went off and spent his money on (as my father would say) wine, women, and song. He eventually went through all the money and ended up working in the fields of other men just so he could eat. He said "when I was with my father, even his servants had enough to eat and yet I am almost starving. I will go back to my father and work as a servant for him". Now mind you the older brother is still working in the fields of his father every day. Doing his best to please his father. The younger brother starts back to his home and the father sees him coming down the road. He starts to rejoice and tells the servants to prepare a great meal and we will feast. Kill the fatted calf (I hate fatty meat) and we will celebrate. My son was dead. And now he is alive again!

Now meanwhile back in the fields the older brother sees what's going on and is more than a little miffed. He approaches his father and says "I have worked for you every day and have never complained. The working conditions are lousy, there is no 401k, and my secretary is ugly as sin. And yet you celebrate the return of the son who disobeyed you. The father said to the eldest son

"Don't you understand! My son was dead to me, and now he lives"! The older brother organized a strike and became the leader of the first chapter of the teamster's union in their town.

What does this parable mean? My interpretation of it is that even though someone strays from God, coming back wipes the slate clean. God forgives easier than most. I myself being an older brother would have started my own union too. That's why I'm not perfect. God let's all who are remorseful for their sins back into his good graces. I suppose that's why he's the big guy. He can do something like that and hold no ill will. Not many of us could do that.

There are a couple of other comments I'd like to make about things in the Bible that have always confused me. We will move on with the New Testament after I get this off of my chest.

Why weren't lambs going extinct in ancient Israel? Every couple of minutes, someone was sacrificing one. Why the bad wrap for Lambs? If you really want to impress me, sacrifice a Lion or a Rhinoceros. That's got to be a very impressive thing to God. Taking out a little Lamb seems kind of wimpy. And even though the lambs were eventually being burned to have their ashes go up to heaven for god, wouldn't it have been better to kill the lamb and give the meat to the poor? How come I've got to think of all this stuff? You paid money for the lamb and brought it to the temple only to have it slaughtered by the priests and burned. What a waist. You also had to pay the priests for the actual sacrifice. Someone's getting rich here and it isn't the average Jewish person in the bible.

The corruption in the Temple was rampant. The priests were great landowners and enjoyed the spoils of being very rich. I'm not saying all of them were this way, some of them I'm sure were there for the right purpose. There are saints hidden all around us. So I'm sure that some of these men were great leaders and holy men. But they all obviously hated lambs. I'm sure if they came home for dinner and the wife had prepared lamb, they probably went out to the local McDonalds and got a Filet of Fish and some fries. McDonalds had to mainly serve kosher dishes in Jerusalem. But they popped up all over once they broke into the market. Even Jesus loved the fries.

Now were getting to the real heart of Christianity. Jesus decides to go to Jerusalem and enter the city riding a donkey. This is known as Palm Sunday because the people of Jerusalem laid down palm tree branches in front of Jesus as he entered the city. This is estimated to have occurred about a week before the resurrection. The symbolism is captured in Zechariah 9:9 "The Coming of Zion's King – See, your king comes to you, righteous and victorious, lowly and riding on a donkey, on a colt, the foal of a donkey". It was perceived that Jesus was declaring he was the King of Israel to the anger of the Sanhedrin. http://en.wikipedia.org/wiki/Jesus_on_a_donkey

Palm Sunday is celebrated the week before Easter in the Christian faith. As I've told you, I was raised catholic. Palm Sunday was the yearly torture for all kids who just wanted to go home and play baseball. The Mass on any given Sunday was anywhere from 45 minutes to an hour long depending upon how much begging the priest had to do during the mass to get the parking lot refinished or announce that the upcoming bake sale would feature one of my Mom's desserts (world famous in our church and the reason why I'll never be on the cover of GQ Magazine). Also, if there was a significant number of sick parishioners we had to pray for the mass could go an hour. By this time my father was giving me one of his looks about fidgeting in my seat and I knew I would receive lecture number 107 (I numbered them after a while. There were so many) in the car on the way home. Lecture 96 involved me eating too many of my mom's desserts during the bake sale and cutting into the profits. Lecture 39 was the "You're going to make us late for mass if you don't get up". This one could involve some physical motivation from my father pulling me out of bed and physically standing me up. Dad was a big fellow, about 6'5" and 260 pounds. A real motivating factor in a child's life. But the one mass I dreaded most was the Palm Sunday Mass. It could easily go an hour and a half with no intermission or popcorn stand. The priest would bless the palms with water and then there would be a little parade with everyone who wanted one taking a little spin around the church like a kid who just got the best gift on Christmas. Of course, I followed in line like a lemming and was happy to get up and stretch my legs. Another thing about the Catholic Church if you're not familiar with it is the constant sitting, then standing, then kneeling. It looks like a large dance troop practicing their moves. And heaven forbid you should be caught with your ass leaning against the seat when you were expected to be kneeling upright. If the Sunday school teacher saw you, you would be assigned some paper on a part of the Old Testament that Jesus himself couldn't understand. If my mom caught you, the evil eye would be pointed your way, and you would quickly get into the proper kneeling position. If Dad caught you lecture number 19 would be given in the car ride home. The Catholics were famous for their expertise in inflicting guilt and my mom and dad were award winners in it. My mother had her black belt in guilt and could get an invading army to turn around and go home just by mentioning that Jesus would be ashamed of them for ruining her new front lawn.

Back to Palm Sunday. The palms were eventually burned to ash and used to decorate the foreheads of all Catholics on Ash Wednesday. This was the reason I walked around school all day with non-Catholic children pointing at my forehead saying, "You've got some dirt on your forehead". You weren't allowed to wash it off until that night before you went to bed in my house. I think that was because Mom didn't want to wash 7 pillowcases in the morning. If I ever do decide to re-enter the Catholic faith my first day back will be Easter Sunday so that I can wait a whole year before having to go to Palm Sunday Mass.

Alright. Here's where we see a different side of Jesus. As Jesus entered the Temple for the first time in Jerusalem something snapped. You know Jesus must have had a pretty even temperament but something so degrading to his father's house made him look like a bull in a china shop. Not that they had China shops back then, or any bulls running through them.

The temple priests had certain rules regarding money.

They only accepted one kind. Roman. Many people had made pilgrimages from far-off lands and would have to have their money converted to the currency the Temple priest used. This is where the term "Moneychangers" comes in. They were in the business of making these exchanges and keeping a lot of the money for themselves. Not a favorable lot. They also sold doves, pigeons and of course the lambs we talked about previously. Jesus is making his way to the temple and sees what's going on and blows a gasket. No one knew what a "Gasket" was so everyone was confused. Jesus uttered some very harsh words. "My house shall be called the house of prayer, but ye have made it a den of thieves." Back then, these were fightin' words partner. Jesus took on the role of Arnold Schwarzenegger and started kicking some moneychanger butt. He is said to have either fashioned a whip out of cord or used a large stick and started overturning the moneychanger's tables, releasing the animals, and calling the temple priest nasty names that his mother Mary admonished him for. (Even Jesus got in trouble with his mother for swearing). After he was done, the place was a shambles. Money everywhere, animals roaming around aimlessly, and the temple priests giving Jesus the evil eye. This was not a good way to get their backing. Jesus from this point on was known as a "Troublemaker" and given detention. He ignored the detention using the "Son of God" excuse and no one called him on it. He said he would tear down the temple and rebuild it in 3 days. I asked several of my construction worker friends if this would be possible and they said it would take at least a couple of weeks just to get the permits. So obviously Jesus was using this as a metaphor referring to his future of dying and being resurrected in three days. But no one got the metaphor and Jesus just looked like he was bragging about his carpenter skills. He is said to have been able to build a very nice table and chairs for rich people. Always good to have something to fall back on if this "son of God" thing doesn't work out. (What is that? Day 27 in purgatory?)

I like the story of the money changers. It shows that Jesus was human during his time on earth. It shows he was capable of all kinds of emotions. Now I'm not one for committing an act of violence to get your point across, but I've done it before. Sometimes it's the only answer. I know that sounds bad, but kicking a little ass once in a while is something humans do.

Unfortunately, this was the beginning of the end for Jesus. Even though he was allowed to preach in the temple and even perform a few miracles, (making the blind see, and healing a nasty case of toenail fungus on one of the high priests) the guards and higher-ups were watching him closely. Especially the highest priest Caiaphas, who had a bad attitude and didn't even want Jesus to look at his toenails. This is where the trouble starts to show itself.

The Last Supper was the final meal Jesus had with his disciples. Jesus ordered a Filet Minion, a double baked potato, and a bottle of champagne from the year 4 B.C. (Very expensive) the disciples decided to pool their money and only have chicken to keep the costs down. If it was going to be my last supper that's what I'd order. The truth is they probably had fruit bread and wine. Maybe some sort of meat if they were lucky. No one was writing down the menu, so it's lost to time. The disciples probably though that this was going to be just another supper with their teacher, but he made it pretty clear after a while that this was a very special meal. He said things like "Take this bread and eat it. For it is my body which is given up for you". Not long after all the apostles had taken the bread Jesus lifted a wine glass and said "This is the cup of my blood. The cup of the new and everlasting covenant. It will be given up for you". Pretty profound words from the teacher. He was teaching them how to preach and started the beginnings of the church services that are given every Sunday throughout Christianity. Jesus then washed the feet of all the apostles and said, "love one another as I have loved you". Washing someone's feet was a big deal back then. So, I'm sure the symbolism in this action is pretty profound. Jesus was getting them already for their journeys to preach his word. There were other amazing revelations revealed at the last supper. By the way the term "The Last Supper" is not in any of the gospels. It was coined years later. Jesus looked at the apostles and said, "one of you will betray me tonight". This started an argument with Thomas doubting what Jesus was saying so he made him go stand in the corner for 15 minutes of time-out. Everyone said they would never betray Jesus but when the time came, Jesus looked at Judas and said, "do what you have to do you lousy snitch"! Alright I added that last part. Judas departs going to the Sanhedrin and telling them for a price of 30 silver coins he would deliver Jesus to them. Judas gets a very bad wrap in the New

Testament and maybe it's well deserved. But there have also been some theory's that Jesus needed someone strong and picked one of his favorite apostles (Judas) to get the ball rolling on the acts that were to follow. Some people think Jesus may have even told Judas about the wrath he would receive from the world but that he was the one Jesus new would do whatever he told him to do for the good of the faith of Christianity. There was also a gospel found that was attributed to Judas in some old scrolls found in the 1970's. They don't know if they are real or fake. The papyrus they were written on dates from no earlier than the second century. It is thought to have been written by some Gnostic followers of Jesus. Its carbon dated to 280 A.D. plus or minus 60 years. It basically says that Jesus taught Judas the "True Gospel" and his teachings were the true words of Jesus. This is a real mess for the entire story of Jesus. Judas is thought to be the bad guy but maybe he was just a cog in the wheel of the big picture. I'm not sure what to believe here. I find when an ancient text is recovered and interpreted it's like a belly button. Everyone has one. The interpretations are vast and very different, but it does make for some interesting arguments. Was Jesus using Judas because he knew he would be strong enough to do what he needed him to do? Was Judas just a jerk who wanted 30 pieces of silver to buy himself some new sandals and clothes? Or is the story of Judas a little bit of both opinions? I'm not sure what to think.

Also, at the last supper Peter said "I would never disobey you, I will follow you to the ends of the earth. (Which back then wasn't thought of as a big ordeal). Jesus said to

Peter "By the time the cock crows, you will have denied knowing me three times". Of course, Peter doesn't believe him because his commitment to Jesus is so great that he thought it would be impossible. But as we find out later in the story, in the heat of the arrest and trial of Jesus, Peter does in fact deny him three times to save his own skin. This Jesus guy was definitely psychic. Being the son of God I'd imagine that isn't much of a feat for him.

So back to the last supper. Jesus finishes up his steak saying, "it was a little tough, but still delicious" and has laid waste to the double-baked potato. Jesus was a real carb man and I think the only thing that kept him from being overweight was all that walking he had to do. Also, Jerusalem isn't famous for its pasta dishes. The group finished up their meal but posed for a picture before the left. Leonardo Di Vinci later used it for his painting "The Last supper". It was slightly out of focus, but Leo still pulled it off. What a masterpiece. Some think Mary Magdalene may have taken the picture. But some also think Mary was sitting next to Jesus in the Painting. Another theory that can get me in trouble.

After the picture, Jesus and his posse went to the garden of Gethsemane to rest for the night. Jesus went off on his own saying he needed to have a talk with "Dad" and asked some of the apostles to stay awake and watch over him as he prayed from a distance. Now at the time you have to remember Jesus was human. He knew what pain and suffering was. He once walked from Nazareth to Bethlehem with a severely sprained ankle and fought through the pain even though Peter had offered to give him a piggyback ride. Jesus had sprained the ankle taking on the roman guards at Nazareth in a pick-up basketball game. Jesus versus the 3rd battalion as it was billed. Jesus won the game with a last-second three-pointer from half-court and sent the battalion packing. The sprain occurred during Jesus's celebration dance after the shot. A lot of people thought Jesus's dad was keeping his ego in check.

In the garden, Jesus began to pray. He asked his father if there might be another way to accomplish this mission. Maybe some billboard advertising or an infomercial. He even promised to do extra chores when he got to heaven if God would just get him out of what was to come. God wasn't buying any of this and Jesus then new his fate was sealed. He went back to his disciples who he had instructed to stay awake and found them all sleeping. Jesus got a bucket of warm water and put all their hands in it until they wet the bed. (Day 28 in purgatory). Jesus admonished them for not doing what they were told and then made them go change their clothes because they all had asparagus at dinner, and they smelled really bad. Jesus went back and tried to get his case heard by a higher court but God said, "Who do you think is the highest court"? Jesus realized the jig was up the news was out they finally found me. (Sorry, big Styx Fan) The Sanhedrin appeared in the garden and Judas walked up to Jesus and kissed him on the cheek. Jesus said, "You betray your master with a kiss". The guards of the Sanhedrin arrested Jesus. Peter gets angry and is said to have chopped off one of the guard's ears during the skirmish. Jesus couldn't let that go and pressed the fallen ear against the guard's head and the ear was miraculously reattached. Jesus told Peter "All who live by the sword will perish by the sword". Peter got the message and dropped the sword. They took Jesus away to the house of Caiaphas. It is assumed that the guards of the Sanhedrin were pretty rough on him and when he appeared before the high priests, he didn't look real good.

Now like I said before there were some supporters of Jesus in the Sanhedrin. Nicodemus being one of them. He had seen some of Jesus's work and had heard him speak. Nicodemus was a forward thinker back then. His argument was "Why not now? Why should we not think that this man could not be the Messiah as he says he is"? Caiaphas didn't buy this story along with the majority of the Sanhedrin. When Caiaphas asked Jesus "Are you the Son of the Living God, The Messiah"? Jesus said, "I am". That cause Caiaphas to rip open his rope which in my opinion was something no one wanted to see. An old man in his underwear has never been a pleasant thing to see even up to this point in history. The Sanhedrin had heard enough, and they condemned Jesus to death. One problem though. Only Rome had the authority to condemn somebody to death. And also, this was the time of the Sabbath and that just complicated things even further. It is assumed that Jesus was held prisoner until the Sanhedrin could talk the roman procurator Pontius "the Hammer" Pilot into doing their dirty work for them.

Pontius Pilot was not known as a kind man. He hated governing the Jewish people and called them many nasty names. Just as a side note not too long after Jesus's death, he was recalled to Rome because of his extreme cruelty to the Jews. Cesar grounded him for a year and Pilot became very angry and started his own torture business contracting his services out to many small groups.

The Sanhedrin brought Jesus to Pilot and asked him if he would put him to death. Pilot asked "what has this man done? Why such a severe punishment?" The Sanhedrin explained to Pilot that Jesus was a blasphemer and must be put to death because he claimed to be the King of the Jews. Now claiming to be a king in a Roman occupied land was a big no no back then. You were saying that you were in control, not the Romans. Back then the whole known world was pretty much under Roman control. So, this got Pilot thinking that this in itself was a pretty serious crime but not enough to be put to death. I think Pilot had seen enough of what they referred to at that time as "False Profits" to know this was just another religious zealot who was a little touched in the head. He offered the Sanhedrin a token of Roman punishment and sent Jesus out to be whipped and beaten. The whips back then had some interesting added punch to them with little iron hooks and even broken pieces of glass or pottery placed in them. If you've ever seen Mel Gibson's "The Passion of the Christ" you will get an idea of how savage this sentence was. In Mel's version, from a medical standpoint, Jesus probably would have died of blood loss long before he got to the cross. The Romans then returned Jesus to Pontius Pilot, and he tried to get Jesus to defend himself against his accusers. When Pilot got angry because Jesus refused to speak, he said "don't you know I have the power to have you crucified"! Jesus looked at him and said, "You would not have that power if it wasn't given to you from above".

So Pilot, not really wanting to put Jesus to death came up with an idea. Although scholars can find no evidence of this tradition anywhere in Roman history, he offered as a token of Roman kindness to free one man who was condemned to death on Passover. Two men were chosen. One being Barabbas and the other Jesus. Barabbas was doing time for passing bad checks and other crimes. (He was the first identity thief, stealing the identity of a Roman soldier and running up his credit cards) and maybe in sighting a riot. Supposedly, Pilot gave the crowd the choice of freeing either Barabbas or Jesus. Barabbas was known to be sort of a revolutionary and hated Rome. His crime may have been as serious as killing a Roman Guard although he would have surely been put to death for that. The Sanhedrin was instrumental in getting the crowd on Barabbas's side and Jesus lost the election. Pilot was not happy. He is said to have "washed his hands of the whole matter" putting the blame fully on the Jewish People. They took Jesus away and Barabbas went free.

The truth about this story is hard to say. The chances of this happening were pretty slim. Pilot would not have let a small crowd of Jews control the outcome of a prisoner's fate. Especially one as volatile as Barabbas. The story does appear in the conical gospels but goes against everything Roman occupation meant in those times. They were in control. Period. Even the Sanhedrin would not have the power to change Pilots mind in this situation. There may be another story, lost to history regarding the actual trial and sentence of Jesus of Nazareth. And we won't know until we cross over to the other side and can ask all the questions we want. They aren't going to like me over there. I've got so many questions about so many things they better find the most patient teacher that has ever lived to sit with me and fill me in on everything from the true beginning of the human race to the Kennedy assassination to why certain old girlfriends left me. All of this is important to me. I hope I can get some answers when I get there.

Sorry, a little off track there. Let's look at the crucifixion from a Roman standpoint. These bastards were more than mean. They were trying to set examples of the enemies of Rome in ways that were not only extremely sick but also quite creative. There was a time in history were over a thousand Jewish people were nailed to the walls surrounding Jerusalem because there was not enough wood to make crosses for everyone. This is more than sick. This is a serious act that must have put the man who thought of the idea in hell sitting next to Hitler and Stalin. I don't know what or if hell is there, but I'd like to think there is some restitution paid to the people who these crimes were committed against. Maybe they get to kill their accusers the same way they were killed. Only seems fair. After all of those people have had their revenge, we can start to talk about forgiveness. Although I'm not sure it would ever happen for such people.

The Romans also had a real talent for torture. Whips, flogging, steel hooks, making prisoners watch bad teenage vampire shows over and over again. The Coliseum was a favorite entertainment spot for Romans. Christians were often sent to their deaths there using anything from gladiatorial combat to throwing them to the lions. Being burned alive was also a favorite of some of the Roman emperors. If you ever get a chance read a little about the Roman emperor Caligula. This was one of the sickest bastards of all time. Nero wasn't much better, and he blamed a big fire in Rome on them even though he is thought to of set the fire himself to make room for a new palace he planned to build. I'm telling you all this, so you understand that Jesus's crucifixion was just one option for the Romans. It was considered to be the most embarrassing for the victim in those times. It could take days for them to die. If the Roman soldiers got tired of waiting, they would take the equivalent of a sledgehammer and break both of the victim's legs to hasten their death. They would suffocate because they could no longer support themselves on the cross.

Jesus's crucifixion was preceded by beatings from both the Sanhedrin guards and priests along with the Roman soldiers. Although it is thought that after these savage beatings, Jesus was forced to carry a full-size cross through the city, out to a hill just outside of the city, and nailed to the cross this would not be streamlined enough for the Romans who were into assembly line crucifixions. It is more likely that Jesus carried only the top of the cross which had been tied to his arms. The route through the city is a pilgrimage that many Christians follow each year although there is some debate as to what the true route was. I won't get into it, but like I said, the romans were into streamlining the process. So, the shortest route would have been taken. The entire time the Romans kept beating Jesus and he fell many times. At one point a bystander to the event was told to help carry the cross. This would get him an automatic "Get out of Jail free" card when he crossed over to heaven. Can you imagine how happy that guy must have been when he realized that he helped the Christ carry his cross? See how acts of kindness can pay off. It is thought that when Jesus reached the hilltop he was thrown to the ground, nailed to the upper part of the cross, and then hoisted up to the support. It was then that his feet were nailed to it. A couple of years ago, a heal bone was found in an archeological dig that actually had a nail driven through it. It suggests that the legs were turned sideways in one direction and the heels were nailed together and into the cross. This would even be more painful than the way Jesus is depicted on the cross in most paintings. The heels are covered with a lot of nerves and some of them would surely have been severed in the process causing great pain.

Jesus lingered on the cross for 6 hours and is thought to have died at approximately 3 P.M. To make sure he was dead, a roman guard speared him in the side. It is said that quite a bit of fluid and blood came out of the wound as it was inflicted. I did see on program (I wish I could remember what it was called) that suggested that the spear may have pierced the pericardium of the heart which may have been filled with blood and fluid. This would suggest that Jesus final cause of death may have been cardiac tamponade. This is a condition where the heart is surrounded by fluid (probably blood and water) that caused his heart to fail. He had been beaten so badly and suffered several falls with a large piece of wood on his back during the crucifixion. If he had fallen on his chest several times, this could have caused the cardiac tamponade. Just a theory from a guy who has worked in the field of cardiology for years.

He may have died of dehydration, shock, blood loss, or any other thing that is brought on by the severe treatment he received. The fact that he lingered for 6 hours makes me believe that Jesus was a superhero. I would have died when they hit me the first time with the whip.

It is said a great storm blew up at the time of Jesus's death scattering the crowd and putting fear into the Roman guards that were responsible for his death. In Mel Gibson's "Passion of the Christ" parts of the temple were destroyed at the time of his death making Caiaphas wet himself. How would you like to be that guy when you crossed over to heaven and saw Jesus standing next to God? How embarrassing. The begging that must have occurred at that time from Caiaphas would have been monumental. I'm sure Jesus forgave him, that's what he does. I on the other hand would have had to have a little revenge. That's why it's a definite fact that I am not the 3rd coming of the savior. Any of you who know me pretty much know that already.

The body of Jesus was released to the family because it was against Jewish law to leave a body outside overnight. There are different accounts in the conical gospels along with many other writers. History is funny that way. The gospel of Mark which is thought to be the earliest of the gospels, says that Joseph of Arimathae, who was not an avid follower of Jesus asked Pontius Pilot if he could have the body so it could be entombed properly under Jewish law. After Pilot allowed Joseph of Arimathae to take the body it was wrapped in linen and laid in a tomb. The tomb (in some accounts) was Joseph of Arimathae's tomb. He was a pious man and allowed the body to be placed there. It is also thought that Joseph was a man of wealth and could afford to build another tomb for himself. It was so close to darkness the body may not have been anointed or cleaned. However in the Gospel of Mark, a woman pours perfume over Jesus before his death which would anoint the body for burial. Also, in the gospel of Mark, it is said that Nicodemus brought the spices to anoint the body. After wrapping it in the linen, Jesus was laid in the tomb. Matthew 27:66 mentions that they "made the tomb secure by putting a seal on the stone and posting the guard." http://en.wikipedia.org/wiki/Burial_of_Jesus

It is thought that the reason Jesus was left in the tomb all day Saturday was to represent the day of rest God took during the creation of the Earth and to prepare for the resurrection. Jesus had a deck of cards and played solitaire almost all-day Saturday. (One more day in purgatory). Jesus resurrects on Sunday. This is now represented in most religions as "Easter Sunday". This has always confused me. We celebrate Easter at least here in the States by imagining a large white bunny breaking into our homes and leaving Easter baskets filled with chocolate and eggs. First things first. Rabbits don't lay eggs. Second, why is chocolate the "Easter treats" we have all been accustomed to? And third, in the deep south of the United States, a large white rabbit breaking into your house would represent rabbit stew for dinner that night. With leftovers galore. It shows you the power advertising has over all of us. Don't get me wrong, I tore into Easter baskets like a fat kid who hadn't eaten in 24 hours, mainly because I was a fat kid who hadn't eaten in at least 12 hours which felt like 24 when you're looking at a basket filled with chocolate. White chocolate was my favorite. That would get devoured first. Followed by Reese's peanut butter eggs and then Hershey's kisses. By the time we went to church, I was lapsing into a diabetic coma.

Now back to the resurrection. In Christianity, the empty tomb is the tomb of Jesus that was found to be empty by the women myrrhbearers who had come to his tomb to carry out their last devotions to Jesus' body by anointing his body with spices and by pouring oils over it.

All four canonical gospels report the incident with significant variations. Jesus' body was laid out in the tomb after crucifixion and death. All the gospels report that women were the first to discover the Resurrection of Jesus. The first hint that something had happened was the rolled-away stone. This stone, as was typical of ancient tombs, had covered the entrance. They found the tomb to be empty, the body is gone, and a young man or angel(s) within the tomb or on the rolled-away stone told the women that Jesus had risen. These accounts lead to beliefs concerning the Resurrection of Jesus, with many Resurrection appearances of Jesus. The empty tomb points to the revelation of Jesus' resurrection, implicitly in the canonical Gospel of Mark (without the later endings) and explicitly in the other three canonical gospel narratives. http://en.wikipedia.org/wiki/Empty_tomb

Now due to the way women were treated back then it was quite a shock to the men that Jesus had appeared to Mary Magdalene and possibly other women first. It might have something to do with the fact that the apostles and disciples were hiding out, afraid that they would be associated with Jesus and crucified too. The women went to anoint the body (there seems to be a lot of anointing in the Jewish faith) and they found the stone overturned and Jesus's body gone. There were several guards posted by both the Sanhedrin and the Romans to guard the tomb since Jesus had proclaimed he would rise from the dead and the Sanhedrin just couldn't allow that to happen. Turns out, God gave the guards a heavy meal of turkey and stuffing with all the fixing and the guards lapsed into turkey comas. Jesus rose from the dead, knocked over the rock like it was a wall built of lego's and waltzed (maybe just walked) out of the tomb. He appeared to Mary Magdeline as she went to anoint the body and said "Why do you look for the living among the dead?" Mary fell to her knee recognizing that the man she was talking to was Jesus. He told her to go tell the other apostles that he had risen. She went to their hiding place and told them her account of what had happened. No one, including Peter believed her at first. She got a little huffy and stormed out not offering to do their laundry or fix them lunch. Mary had had enough of these men and is not mentioned again in the New Testament.

As you can imagine, there are differing accounts of this story. The conical gospels can't even agree upon it. The different accounts are listed below. Pick one.

<u>According to Mark, Mary Magdalene, Mary the mother of James, and Salome finds that the tomb has been opened.</u>

When the Sabbath was over, Mary Magdalene, Mary the mother of James, and Salome bought spices so that they might go to anoint Jesus' body. Very early on the first day of the week, just after sunrise, they were on their way to the tomb and they asked each other, "Who will roll the stone away from the entrance of the tomb?" But when they looked up, they saw that the very large stone had been rolled away. As they entered the tomb, they saw a young man dressed in a white robe sitting on the right side, and they were alarmed. "Don't be alarmed," he said. "You are looking for Jesus the Nazarene, who was crucified. He has risen! He is not here. See the place where they laid him. But go, tell his disciples and Peter, 'He is going ahead of you into Galilee. There you will see him, just as he told you.'" Trembling and bewildered, the women went out and fled from the tomb. They said nothing to anyone because they were afraid.

<u>According to Matthew, an angel in shining garments is seen by Mary and Mary opening the tomb, and the angel tells them not to be afraid since Jesus *is risen from the dead:*</u>

After the Sabbath, at dawn on the first day of the week, Mary Magdalene and the other Mary went to look at the tomb.

There was a violent earthquake, for an angel of the Lord came down from heaven and, going to the tomb, rolled back the stone and sat on it. His appearance was like lightning, and his clothes were white as snow. The guards were so afraid of him that they shook and became like dead men. The angel said to the women, "Do not be afraid, for I know that you are looking for Jesus, who was crucified. He is not here; he has risen, just as he said. Come and see the place where he lay. Then go quickly and tell his disciples: 'He has risen from the dead and is going ahead of you into Galilee. There you will see him.' Now I have told you.

The women hurried away from the tomb, afraid yet filled with joy, and ran to tell his disciples. Suddenly Jesus met them. "Greetings," he said. They came to him, clasped his feet, and worshiped him. Then Jesus said to them, "Do not be afraid. Go and tell my brothers to go to Galilee; there they will see me."

<u>According to Luke, the women discover the tomb has been opened, and two men in shining garments come up to them and tell them not to be afraid since Jesus *is risen*.</u>

On the first day of the week, very early in the morning, the women took the spices they had prepared and went to the tomb. They found the stone rolled away from the tomb, but when they entered, they did not find the body of the Lord Jesus. While they were wondering about this, suddenly two men in clothes that gleamed like lightning stood beside them. In their fright the women bowed down with their faces to the ground, but the men said to them, "Why do you look for the living among the dead? He is not here; he has risen! Remember how he told you, while he was still with you in Galilee: 'The Son of Man must be delivered into the hands of sinful men, be crucified and on the third day be raised again." Then they remembered his words.

The gospel of John contains the most complete narrative including the appearance of Jesus:

Early on the first day of the week, while it was still dark, Mary Magdalene went to the tomb and saw that the stone had been removed from the entrance. So, she came running to Simon Peter and the other disciple, the one Jesus loved, and said, "They have taken the Lord out of the tomb, and we don't know where they have put him!" Peter and the other disciples started for the tomb. Both were running, but the other disciple outran Peter and reached the tomb first. He bent over and looked in at the strips of linen lying there but did not go in. Then Simon Peter, who was behind him, arrived and went into the tomb. He saw the strips of linen lying there, as well as the burial cloth that had been around Jesus' head. The cloth was folded up by itself, separate from the linen. Finally, the other disciple, who had reached the tomb first, also went inside. He saw and believed. (They still did not understand from Scripture that Jesus had to rise from the dead.)

Then the disciples went back to their homes, but Mary stood outside the tomb crying. As she wept, she bent over to look into the tomb and saw two angels in white, seated where Jesus' body had been, one at the head and the other at the foot. They asked her, "Woman, why are you crying?" "They have taken my Lord away," she said, "and I don't know where they have put him." At this, she turned around and saw Jesus standing there, but she did not realize that it was Jesus.

By comparison, the apocryphal Gospel of Peter describes two men carrying a third out of the tomb, with a cross following them and speaking:

And in the night in which the Lord's Day was drawing on, as the soldiers kept guard two by two in a watch, there was a great voice in the heaven; and they saw the heavens opened, and two men descend with a great light and approach the tomb. And the stone that was put at the door rolled off itself and made way in part; and the tomb was opened, and both the young men entered.

When therefore those soldiers saw it, they awakened the centurion and the elders, for they too were close by keeping guard. And as they declared what things they had seen, again they saw three men come forth from the tomb, and two of them supporting one, and a cross following them. And the heads of the two reached to heaven, but the head of him who was led by them overpassed the heavens. And they heard a voice from the heavens, saying, you have preached to them that sleep. And a response was heard from the cross, Yes.

http://en.wikipedia.org/wiki/Empty_tomb

Now remember, these are the 4 conical gospels (approved for the New Testament by the council of Nicaea) along with Peter's account. As you see all of them are different, especially Peter's account which is way out there. There are other gospels too. The Gnostic gospels (there are many, but the ones that get mentioned the most are the Gospel of Mary, The Gospel of Thomas, Gospel of Truth, Gospel of Philip, and the Gospel of Judas. I'm not sure if any of them mention the resurrection. These gospels were mostly found in the late 1800's and were not in good condition. Some of them being stored in sealed jars in the dessert or in caves. What has been made out of them is interesting reading. Including the part that mentions that Mary Magdalene was a favorite of Jesus and he often kissed her on the ____________. The last word is missing in the text. Your guess is as good as mine although a lot of scholars say the missing word is mouth. This would lend credence to the story that Mary was more than just a disciple. Again, if you want that version of the story, watch the Di Vinci code by Dan Brown. It may be a novel, but there are a lot of facts in it too.

So, we have several accounts. All written at least 60 to 90 years after the death and resurrection of Jesus. This just complicates things. Sometimes I think they should have picked one gospel and stuck with it. The book wouldn't be so heavy, and we would all agree on it. Or at least some of us would.

Jesus stayed on earth for 40 days after the resurrection. There's those 40 days thing again. I just don't get it. What is the special meaning of 40 days? Is it because of the original story of Moses wandering in the desert or something else? 40 days, 40 years, 40 everything. Another question I have to ask the big guy when I get upstairs.

When Jesus does reappear to the apostles guess what happened? You guessed it. Thomas has a problem with the whole "coming back to life thing". Jesus made him stick his fingers in the holes in his hands and the wound in his side. Thomas fell to his knees and said, "they should call me doubting Thomas from now on" and the name stuck. Jesus is said to have filled his disciples with the Holy Spirit and sent them of to preach that the coming of the son of God had been fulfilled. They split up and went to many foreign lands. Jesus remained on earth for a number of days after that and could be seen at the Sea of Galilei working on his tan. He signed a few autographs and read the paper. God finally said, "that's enough of that, son. Now get up here, I have work for you to do". Jesus had been gone so long that God had a whole list of chores for him to do.

Actually, in two gospels only the ascension is mentioned. Luke and Mark. Mark says they were eating and Jesus said, "Go out and teach the gospels as I have taught you" and then he ascended into heaven. Luke's version is a little more elaborate. Jesus took the 11 apostles to Bethany. He lifted up his hands and blessed them and then was carried off to heaven by a Lear jet with God at the helm. The Flight attendant was very nice and served Jesus wine and bread and gave him a warm cloth napkin when he was done.

I've decided to stop here. At the ascension. Because in my mind, that's when all the excitement is finalized, and the rest of the New Testament is very complex and involves many writers with many opinions and rules that they attribute to God. Sort of a divine intervention. They were told by God to write this stuff down and spread the word. The thing that I can't get past is the rules and regulations put forth from this point on. There is quite a bit about fasting. This must have been practiced quite often back then. I know in several denominations; it is still practiced. I don't understand it. It would not help me get closer to God. It would just make me angry. When I don't eat, I get cranky. This would make my prayer to God filled with unimportant things like "Where are the Twinkies, God? And could you make a filet minion magically appear? If I had eaten, I would be more interested in asking for help for the poor and the sick. I always am better on a full stomach.

What else do I have to say? Well, I struggle with re-ligion. I have for years. I see preachers on TV begging for money, mostly to improve the church and TV programs they produce. They write books that are inspirational to some and make a pretty profit off of them. Some of them are good people. The only one I do like is Joel Osteen. He seems to be more interested in teaching how loving one another and doing your best to help out the less fortunate is the true meaning of Christianity. I've read some of his books and enjoyed them. Even the parts where he gets a little "preachy" for me are tolerable. So, my hat's off to him. He has a huge following and will probably get a free pass into heaven. Some of the other ones I'm not so sure about. Why does God have to be a vengeful, nasty God? Earlier in this book I mentioned that the God of the Old Testament reminded me of my father when I was young. He was strict, sometimes even nasty about his rules. He was a man who didn't take crap from anyone including his children. But like the God of the New Testament, as he aged, he got more mellow. He seemed to be more tolerant and realized that we sometimes had to fall on our faces to learn a lesson. He didn't need to intervene. Then when he had grandchildren, things started to change. While I was trying to set some rules for my kids and give them the boundaries they needed he would come over and feed them candy and then leave. My wife and I then spent several hours trying to get them down off their sugar high and into bed. He stopped yelling and became a man of few words. But when he said something, it was pretty profound or incredibly funny. He had learned to laugh at himself, the situation he was in, even at his illness before he died. I think God will not destroy the earth. I believe we can handle that on our own. He will just sit on his lazy boy (I think God has gotten past the "throne thing") and watch us screw things up. When we all get upstairs, he'll be shaking his head saying things like "didn't I tell you about global warming" and "You knew some nut bag would set off a nuclear weapon, why didn't you get rid of all of them"?

In the New Testament I have at home a couple of pages were stuck together and I found this little-known passage on the newly revealed page.

A letter from Paul to the Corinthians

Dear Corinthians,

This is Paul. How have you been? Things are busy here and I must say this whole Jesus thing is really taking off. I knew he was special, but WOW! How's things by you? Busy? I hope you are all doing well and I plan to visit soon. I'm scheduling a vacation in August, and I hope it's not too hot there. If you could arrange a site seeing tour, I would really appreciate it. How's your camel running? I know you were having trouble getting him started before and talked about getting a new one. As expensive as the new models are, I hope you were able to fix the old one.

Well, I have to go now. I have more letters to write. Everyone seems to like my letters. Maybe someday, they'll put a collection of them together in a book.

Sincerely,

Paul

P.S. Don't forget to tithe, we're trying to start a church.

Well, it's always nice to find new writings in the bible. I hope I'm thought of as a great discoverer of this new document and hailed throughout the Christian world as a great archeologist. (I feel another lightning bolt coming on).

So obviously Paul has written letters that were much more profound than that one, but it is one I can relate to. Paul just wanted to know everything was alright and that he was getting along just fine. Paul is my confirmation name, I don't remember why I chose it, but it might have been because of the previous letter. Some of you will have trouble finding it in your Bibles, but I'm sure if you find just the right version, it will be there right next to the letter "From Peter to Toyota". Peter commented on many things. He liked his Toyota because it was good in the sand, but he had problems with the air conditioning. I'll see if I can find the letter and I'll put it in the book. Don't hold your breath.

Growing up Catholic

From the time I was a little tyke church was a must-do

activity. Democracy at our house was crushed by the rebellion of 1965 when I first asked why I had to go to church. My Dad was the leader of the rebellion and quickly turned the house into a dictatorship. He thought he was the leader but as I look at it now, many years later, he was a puppet dictator. My Mom held the strings and he responded appropriately. The question I asked was forbidden from that point until I was 18 and rebelled against the man. He was older and tired. I told him he could still have the title of dictator, but I would now be my own independent province. I was rather large at 18, so I qualified for my own zip code. My Mom still gave me the silent treatment and brought false accusations in the U.N. regarding my past as a bed wetter. I vehemently denied these charges, but she produced pictures of the sheets into evidence from 1966. I pleaded the fifth from that point out and was ostracized and called names. My island started to attract other bedwetters and the whole place smelled awful after a while. I defected to a small town in Illinois after I gave up control of the island. Boy, that got way out of hand.

So, what do I remember? I went to a church in Markam, Illinois called St. Gerard Majella. Who was St. G as I used to like to call him? He was the patron Saint of expectant mothers which explains a lot. I am the oldest of 5 kids, and I'm pretty sure there would have been more if my mom could have had more. St. Gerard Majella was born in 1726 and died in 1755 of tuberculosis at the age of 29. He would pray for all expectant mothers and was known for his wisdom in counseling women. I'm not sure how a priest counsel's women, but he must have been good at it. After all these years, this is the first time I actually looked up Saint Gerard Majella, I feel some catholic guilt coming on for waiting that long. I'll take a Xanax and it will pass. Plus, I get to see all the pretty colors when I do.

I remember a priest named Father Heffernan. I'm not sure if that's the correct spelling and because of his advanced age when I was a little kid, I'm sure he's with God now. He was a sweet little old man that people listened to when he was saying mass. He would come into the classroom of our CCD program and tell us nice stories and always seemed to be a gentle man of God. He is what I would call a "True man of God". He was a good listener and seemed to relate to all ages. Even when I was older and his health was failing, we still looked forward to his sermons and it's the only time I wouldn't get the evil eye from my mother because I was actually sitting still, listening to this wonderful man. He started his service to the Catholic Church in 1932 and lived to be 89. Father Heffernan was appointed pastor of St. Gerard Majella Church in Markham, Illinois in 1958. I was born in 1961. We didn't move to St. Gerard Majella church until 1965. He was the head of the church at this time. When you're a child, your perception of "Old" is out of whack. When I was a teenager, my parents seemed old. Not that I have teenagers, I'm still young although certain parts of my body would disagree. (My knees! Get your mind out of the gutter). I now have gray hair and walk slower than I use to. Just like my parents did at my age.

St. Gerard Majella was a very pretty church. Big enough

to handle the crowd on Easter and Christmas, but yet small enough to make you feel like you weren't lost in a sea of people. My Dad eventually became a Deacon, which made him even more special in the eyes of the church. He would give out communion, help the priests, and perform miracles every day. The specific miracle was getting me out of bed in the morning for school. I'm sure he will be canonized someday for the frequency of this miracle along with putting up with my sisters' teenage years. I hope it doesn't go to his head up there in heaven. My Mom will be rolling her eyes and saying things like "Oh, look out, here comes the new pope! He thinks his shit doesn't smell". Sorry Dad, just telling it like it is.

It was always interesting approaching the altar during communion when my Dad was up there. My Dad stood about 6'5" and weighed about 260 or so. Father Heffernan was about 5'5" and was a slight man. The two of them looked like the biggest mismatch of the century up there. If I was mad at my dad for something, I would go to Father Heffernan for communion, if we were on good terms I would go to him. We would do the old "Frisbee trick" and most of the time it worked. I could catch the host in my mouth even if his throw was off a little. We never dropped it because that was a disaster in the Catholic Church. Dropping the host on the ground is like dropping the F-bomb during your valedictorian speech. Something I never experienced. My brother Keith was Valedictorian, I wasn't in line for the extra brain power up in heaven. I got the beer-drinking gene instead. Far too many dead brain cells to pass algebra at any level.

In the catholic church, you start to edge towards acceptance by achieving the knowledge needed to complete all your sacraments. The first is baptism. I remember swimming around the little baptism pool in my birthday suit impressing all involved. I got out and ran up and down the aisles yelling "Streaker in the house" and was quickly corralled by my father who apologized to the priest. The priest said to my father "You better watch this one, he's going to be trouble". God new I was a free spirit and quickly forgave me. He even had a little chuckle when I went up into the balcony and played a Beatles song on the church organ. I knew they were going to be big even before they hit America. My Mom grounded me until I was six months old, which was no big deal being that I was still the most famous baby in Saint Gerard Majella church history.

Confession is next in the sacraments. You make your first confession just before your first communion. Confession is just like it sounds. You confess your "Sins" to the priest in a scary little room with a sliding window that slightly obscured your identity. But you knew deep down inside that the priest knew who was in the box and if your sins were of biblical proportions the looks you would receive from the priest for the next couple of weeks were usually pretty telling. My first confession was pretty uneventful. What do you have to confess at the age of 7? I told him I had disrespected my mom and dad, I had used some swear words after striking out in several baseball games, and being that I hadn't discovered my penis yet, that was about it. I felt pretty ripped off so I decided to make some stuff up. I confessed to the Lindberg baby kid-napping and said I had mob ties and was a hitman who had killed several people but they were all bad. I also said I was the second shooter on the grassy knoll. The priest caught on with that one and quickly assigned a number of Hail Mary's and several Our Fathers. I went to the nearest church pew feeling that the confession would keep the priest off my back for a while with the hitman comment. Not so much. He kept me under scrutiny for the rest of my catechism career. Although my mom used to bug me about going to confession, I rarely went. I would ask God to forgive me and felt that was enough. Cut out the middleman that's what I always say. If I had to go today, the conversation would start with me saying "Bless me father for I have sinned, it's been 3 decades since my last confession. You're going to be here a while". The priest would have to pull up a lazy boy recliner, get a drink, and would need a calculator to keep track of my penance. Not that I'm a terrible human being, it just that a lot of stuff can happen over three decades. You also receive a rosary before your confession if I remember right. A rosary is a necklace that is rarely worn, but held closely, especially by the elderly in church. Each bead represents a prayer, most of them are Hail Mary's. There are special beads that require other prayers and being that it has been so long since I've used one, I've forgotten what they are. If you go to a catholic wake, you often find the rosary wrapped around the dead person's hands. It helps keep their hands together and shows everyone that they are a very holy person. This is not always true, but it's a nice touch. I'm sure some very mean people have been given this rosary upon their death and I'm surprised it doesn't burn through the body. I probably shouldn't say this, but my grandma was one of those people. She was a person who pitted her own children against each other for affection, rarely held or cared for her grandchildren, and sometimes made my mother's life a living hell. Now I must say I only knew her when she was old and kind of crabby. She may have been different when she was young. Although some of the family stories would point to that as fiction. She was an avid church goer, so maybe she was trying to make amends for this near the end of her life. I guess you can't like everyone in this life. A funny story here about my dad's sense of humor. My grandfather who was a very funny man who always had a smile for his grandchildren and enjoyed their company died when I was 18. I'm reminded of the joke "Why do men die before their wives? Because they want to". At my grandma's wake my dad came up to me and said "what do you think grandpa Bill is thinking now"? I said, "I don't know, Dad what's he thinking"? My dad replied, "Well at least I had 20 good years in Heaven". I love to laugh. I do it whenever possible. But there are times when laughter is frowned upon. One of them being at a wake. I had to leave the room and laugh outside. I have a feeling my grandpa heard the joke and had a good laugh himself. I can still see the rosary around my grandma's hands. I hope she had that thing smoking before she died. She had a lot to answer for when she crossed over.

Confession was a necessity before you died. Unfortunately, a lot of people don't get that opportunity. I've known people in my life who checked out unexpectedly. I find it hard to believe that they are denied entrance into heaven because they didn't go to confession before they died. A good person is a good person. It shouldn't matter if you didn't get the chance to get your sins forgiven before you die. We all make mistakes. I think God knows that. As George Carlin said, "I can't see some guy doing an eternity in hell for eating a beef jerky on a Friday during Lent". I think we should all concentrate on being good people every day and not fly off the handle at someone and then think "I'll just go to confession, and everything will be O.K.". I have had bosses that treated people like shit all week but would go to church every Sunday and think all their transgressions were forgiven because they helped with the bake sale after the mass. Wrong. Being an asshole all week and assuming you will be forgiven because you'll talk to a priest and be forgiven is just absurd. Here's an idea! Try not to be an asshole. I think God will appreciate it a lot more.

My Mom was a big picture taker when we were kids. Although her aim would have gotten her killed in the Old West, she did her best to document all the special occasions in the house. I have a picture of me in my little red tie, bible in hand, walking down the aisle to make my first communion. Something I'm sure God is reviewing right now. "How'd we let this one slip by, Jesus"? What I do remember about it was we had a lot of serious studying to do to make our first communion. Learning about Saints, Jesus's trials and tribulations, and God's promise to put us in hell if we didn't wear our little red tie. The girls got it even worse. They had the white dress with the fancy veil that blew all over the place in the wind.

What I remember is the party my parents had afterward. I took in enough money to invest in Apple computers and now I'm a multi-millionaire or I bought a 10-speed bike. Being that Apple has no record of me as a shareholder I'm pretty sure it was the bike. I believe I wrecked the bike within a month or two jumping ramps. At the time, K-Mart bikes were not known for their high quality. But I digress. My communion was a very special moment in my parents' life. I guess it was in mine too. At least at the time. You felt like one of the adults going up for communion every week. However, I do have one complaint. Absolutely terrible tasting hosts. If they can make flavored tums now, why can't they make the hosts flavored? It would make communion a little more exciting. "What flavor am I going to get this week"? (Another day in purgatory, which I don't believe in anymore. I hope I'm right because if I'm wrong, I'm going to have to get a long-term lease on an apartment).

Communion is probably the most important of the sacraments. It represents your acceptance into the church as an adult who has made the decision to accept Jesus's as the Son of God. Very important in the Christian faith. Not believing that will get you a ruler across the knuckles in Sunday school. Or at least it used too. My beliefs have changed slightly over the years. I still believe that Jesus was the son of God. But I also believe that over the years God has sent down other Sons and daughters to follow the same path Jesus did. Some of them performed visible miracles, some were just extraordinary people who changed the world for the better. Some of them are now saints, others are people who have no real affiliation with the catholic church but are what I would consider game-changers in the world. Gandhi, Nelson Mandela, Martin Luther King, Jr., Mother Theresa, Buddha, Mohammed, the guy who invented air conditioning (Very important to the extra-large people of the world), Pope John Paul II, and I'm sure there are many more. Why would God only send down one-person 2000 years ago and then leave the rest of the generations without someone special? I think each generation has children of God in it. Maybe they are not well known, but people over the years have been responsible for saving hundreds if not thousands of lives. They sometimes risked their own lives to do this and sometimes lost their lives in the process. George Washington wasn't perfect but think of what he helped start. Abraham Lincoln got the ball rolling on saving an entire race from slavery. Ben Franklin talked about the benefits of Beer. What about the people who won Congressional Medals of Honor? They saved lives at the risk of losing their own, and some of them did. What about the Nurse or Doctor who helped save the life of someone like Albert Einstein when he was very sick? I know some of these are a stretch, but I feel like so many people are truly put on this earth as a gift from God. He made my wife just for me. She has saved me mainly from myself so many times she should be sainted. Even me. My day job is performing Cardiac Ultrasound on Babies that are born with heart defects. I've been doing it for 30 years. I'd like to think that I've saved quite a few babies from an early death. I have friends who are physicians that I've watched sit with a patient during a crisis just so they could be there to save their life if necessary. None of us are perfect, but I think that we all have a little bit of that "Savior" in us. Well not everyone. I've had some bosses over the years that were put on this earth to make people's life miserable. But in general, most people want to do right by God or whatever power they believe in. Maybe God takes on many forms. A tribe in Africa that is isolated from society may believe in a God that is immensely different than the one we're used to. Does that make them wrong? It's what they know. If they serve others and are loved by the rest of the tribe, why would God not acknowledge them too?

Confirmation is basically a recharge of baptism. It is to strengthen and deepen the belief in being accepted into the Catholic Church. All I know is I got an extra name when it was all over. It is customary to pick the name of a Saint. I was going to go with Mary, but it just didn't flow, and I knew my friends would give me hell for it. In the end, I decided on Paul. Paul was considered an apostle but was not one of the original 12. He was instrumental in developing the New Testament and is said to have written 14 of the 27 books of it. Again, this is up for grabs when it comes to the scholars. Paul lived in the same era that Jesus did and some of his writings were thought to be from oral history written down years after Paul's death. I guess I picked Paul because he had the guts to preach to the Romans even when it was against their laws. It eventually cost him his life. It is thought that he was beheaded by

Nero the Emperor. Again, I don't really remember why I picked Paul. Maybe I just thought it sounded good with my name. Confirmation is another reason for a party in the catholic home. It usually happens in 8th grade, and I asked for a hooker as my present. (I had found my penis by then). My Dad had no comment on the idea but deep down I think he may have thought it wasn't such a bad idea. My Mom on the other hand was completely against it. I remember getting another bike, probably another K-Mart special, due to the fact that it was cheap. My Dad didn't believe in quality items, he believed in "the lowest price wins." This was an ongoing theme throughout his life. I did receive cash from other relatives and probably spent it on candy and chocolate milk. Chocolate milk was second in line if Jesus couldn't get wine for the Last Supper. Very few people know this fact. Now you do. You should feel special. Cows were not in great supply back then not to mention the shortage of Hershey's chocolate. That's why they went with wine.

Confirmation was the official end of my catechism career at Saint Gerard Majella church. I'd like to say I was disappointed, but God would get me for a blatant lie. I was done. I had had enough. I continued to go to church. At least for my freshman and sophomore years of high school. When I got my driver's license, I got in the habit of driving around until mass was over and then going to get the weekly mass newspaper (I don't remember what it was called) and go home. This worked well until one of the priests told my dad he hadn't seen me in months. Dad then insisted that I ride with him to church. That went on until

I got a job that required me to work Sunday mornings at a golf course.

Matrimony is the next sacrament. It is preceded by classes and confession to get you ready for the honeymoon in which many of the sins of the church are violated. I remember a little about the classes. A couple who looked like they had only been married a couple of years themselves gives you advice on how to keep a marriage together. Most of it was good information although the part about how you were ostracized for getting a divorce was a little unsettling. Catholic people have to go through quite an ordeal to get divorced and remain in the good graces of the church. They can sometimes get an annulment, which is like getting a "get out of Jail" free card. Otherwise, you are pretty much looked down upon. I think this is incredibly wrong. Some marriages just don't work. People change. People cheat. Sometimes people just grow apart. Why should the spouse who was innocent in the manner be punished? By the spouse, I mean the woman. She's usually the one who takes the most heat for it. Even if the guy gets caught cheating, it somehow becomes her fault that she didn't keep him "Happy" enough to keep the marriage going. I can't tell you how many of my parent's friends lived in incredibly unhappy marriages because divorce was not allowed in the church. Some of them stayed together for the kids, which is not a good reason to keep a marriage going when it's already lost. All the kids get out of it is watching Mom and Dad fight all the time. Sometimes they even get to watch Dad hit Mom, and that gives them a lifetime pass to Psychotherapy. I don't think children are better off with parents like this. They'd be better off with one parent. My parents' marriage was volatile at times. I, being the oldest, caught a lot of the wrath of this anger. I only heard them talk about splitting up once, and in the process of the argument, both parties said, "you're not leaving me with all these damn kids". But then after things cooled down, they cut each one of us down the middle and split us up that way. My bandage was huge! Actually, after my Mom's usual "I'm not speaking to your father" time allotment, they were at least civil to each other. I never doubted that they loved each other, I just couldn't understand why you would want to stay with someone that at times would make you want to jump off a bridge. My Mom was hard to live with mainly because of the rough childhood she had, including catholic grade school and a mother who should have had no kids instead of 8. My Dad wasn't always a peach either. He was a Marine and believed in that form of discipline in raising children. He also could fly of the handle at the smallest thing. So, the two of them together were sometimes like oil and water. Later in their lives they tolerated each other, and maybe even learned to respect each other's little quirks. Although my mom couldn't stand the fact that he was losing his hearing. They were ten years apart in age, but it never showed until they got older. She still had energy to go places and he just wanted to stay home and work on crossword puzzles. His health was not great either. My Dad died at 80. They were married for 50 years. That's like half a century! Why I'm going on with this is to show you that when you lose someone after all those years, sometimes it's impossible to adjust. On my parents 51st anniversary and what also was my Dad's birthday, my Mom went to the Cemetery to deliver a love note saying how much she missed him. It was cold out and my mother had some difficulty breathing in the cold. She left the grave site and got into the car to go back home. She never made it out of the cemetery. She crashed her car after having a heart attack or a pulmonary embolism and died in the cemetery. She was only 70. I'm pretty sure that my dad was tired of making his own milkshakes in heaven (Dad loved my mom's milkshakes) and wanted her up there with him. I'm pretty sure she was happy to go. She was having a real rough time with his death. So, she was only alone for six months. I guess when you truly love someone, no matter what you go through, that love comes through even in the end. My wife Eileen does not visit grave sites. She doesn't like to remember people that way and feels that the person really isn't there. They are in heaven. Although I'm pretty sure she'll visit mine, just to dance on it.

The last sacrament I'm familiar with in the Catholic Church is the anointing of the sick. This is when you're on your last leg and death is imminent. It is helpful if you are still alive and can confess your sins but a lot of times, that's not a possibility. The priest can anoint you and forgive your sins (Supposedly) and you get the bee line to heaven. I have a problem with this. What happens to the poor person who drops dead in the street of a heart attack? They have to go through the punishment of their sins why the guy who had the chance to be anointed and ask that his sins be forgiven gets a free ride? Sorry, I don't buy it.

I think everyone gets a life review when they get to heaven. Maybe you and God sit in side-by-side recliners and watch your life on a big-screen TV. God points out the mistakes, shows you what you should have done instead, and also answers the questions you have like "Why did she dump me when I was so in love with her" and "Why did my boss hate me so much". Any question you can think of about your life gets answered. God doesn't get to upset unless you were a hitman or a mass murderer. Then I think the recliner may have some special tools attached to it to make you feel the pain you caused others. But I think most of us just get a good talking too for the bad things we did and then God forgives us, and we get our assignment for heaven. Maybe you were good on earth with kids. God will make you the greater of small children who pass away. You will keep them happy as you did on earth with the children you knew.

Maybe you were good with finances. God will put you in charge of the budget for some particular aspect of heaven. Maybe you issue company credit cards to specific saints and monitor their spending. You send them emails to warn them that they're near their limit. You could also calculate trips back to earth and the money needed for that soul to get through another life. You know I'm just making this shit up, right?

Musicians would be responsible for entertaining for the Friday night concert. Each Friday a deceased artist performs for all the souls. John Lennon, Jimi Hendrix,

Janis Joplin, A super band with John Panozzo from Styx, Freddie Mercury playing piano and singing, Lead guitar Eddie Van Halen, one of the many rhythm guitarists and John Entwistle from the Who on bass. Can you imagine? I'd try to get a front-row seat every night.

Great actors and actresses putting on plays or producing movies that are all Academy Award winners. Entertainment at its finest every night. Now mind you this is what I think heaven may be like. You may have other ideas. I also have an idea about a personal Harem, but I won't get into that now. But boy is it great!

It's a legitimate question. Is there sex in heaven? It is a very enjoyable part of being mortal so why shouldn't it be available in heaven? I would just like to warn my high school cheerleading squad before they get there. And Sandra Bullock too. I hope my wife skips over this session but if you see me with bruises, it will be obvious she read it.

The End
I'm Probably Going to Hell for This
By
Scott Moss

~ 2 ~

I'd like to dedicate this book
to my father.
he's up in heaven right
now shaking his head.

~ 2 ~